A Student Of Life

SALLY STIERHOFF

WESTBOW
PRESS®
A DIVISION OF THOMAS NELSON
& ZONDERVAN

WestBow Press books may be ordered through booksellers or by contacting:

WestBow Press
A Division of Thomas Nelson & Zondervan
1663 Liberty Drive
Bloomington, IN 47403
www.westbowpress.com
844-714-3454

Interior Image Credit: Shelly Stout

ISBN: 978-1-6642-6957-6 (sc)
ISBN: 978-1-6642-6959-0 (hc)
ISBN: 978-1-6642-6958-3 (e)

Library of Congress Control Number: 2022911425

Print information available on the last page.

WestBow Press rev. date: 07/12/2022

Contents

In Memory of Mark Stierhoff

My husband, Mark, died while I was finishing this book, so in memory of him and all that he brought to my life, I want to acknowledge his contributions. He was a gift from God to me. This book would not be anything like it is if I had not married this wonderful man and experienced so many things with him over the years. God guided us to each other; then we grew in our faith together. I am so very grateful for the life Mark gave me and for the children. I am thankful for his contributions and advice on this book.

Thank you, love, until we meet again in that heavenly realm.

Dedication

I dedicate this book first to my Lord and Savior, Jesus Christ. The relationship I have developed through my faith in Him has sustained me through many challenging times in my life.

Second, I dedicate this book to my husband and our four grown children and their families. I also dedicate it to my extended families and my wonderful friends.

You may ask why I dedicate this book to so many people. It is because I have learned from them and even more people who have come in and out of my life. All my relationships and experiences have made me who I am today. They all have taught me what I'm about to share with you in the pages of this book.

So I thank You and give You praise, Lord. I thank my cherished family and friends as well; you know who you are. God has blessed me so much, and I am eternally grateful for having you in my life.

Preface

A Student of Life is a book that will challenge you. It will encourage deeper spiritual thought and discussion. Wisdom comes to us from time spent with the Lord and in His Word, the Holy Bible. It also comes from a willingness to evaluate and learn from our experiences.

As a student of life, the Lord has revealed many wonderful things to me, and I am compelled to share what I have learned with you. Maybe by doing so, you will have an easier road to travel.

As iron sharpens iron, so one person sharpens another. (Proverbs 27:17)

Acknowledgments

I would love to recognize the many people who have advised me, reviewed and proofed my manuscript, and supplied me with beautiful artwork. Without their hard work and dedication to the Lord, this book would not have been possible. I thank them from the bottom of my heart. I pray this book glorifies the Lord and that His presence is felt when it is read. May the name of the Lord be praised:

Marge Bailey, Pastor Mark Burd, Dr. Wayne Cordeiro, Pastor Steve S. Harman ThD, Pam Henry, Heather Hunt, Kimber Lee Kinney, Debbie Purk, Mark Stierhoff, and Shelly Stout.

Introduction

Oh, how I wish I could go back in time and give this book to my younger self. It would have helped me tremendously. But I guess I had to go through many things in order to learn some valuable life lessons.

This book may be a little different than others. It is filled with chapters on everything from raising a blended family to prayer. It is a kaleidoscope of compositions that will bring the reader a literary picture of what walking through life in the presence of the Lord can look like.

My first book, *SOAP How to Clean Up Your Stinking Thinking One Day at a Time,* was simple and straightforward. While writing *A Student of Life,* I found myself struggling as I tried to put this book into a format similar to other books on the market. I felt so boxed in. It squelched my creativity to the point that I almost quit writing. After some time, I felt the Lord remind me that I was uniquely made, not like anyone else, so my book should be created in the same manner. This revelation allowed me the freedom to express myself as I felt the Lord directed.

In this book I share fictional stories, observations, experiences, poems, and a few of my favorite quotes from other people. I may even use a scripture or a phrase more than once if it fits into the subject that I am writing about. My goal is to inspire and encourage you, the reader, to evaluate your life, establish meaningful relationships, and to truly understand how much God loves you.

Most of us have to face consequences because of our poor decisions. But take heart; it is never too late to turn and start on a new path. "Because of the Lord's great love we are not consumed, for His compassions never fail. They are new every morning; great is Your faithfulness" (Lamentations 3:22–23).

The secret to our success is in knowing ourselves and our Creator. It's also in understanding our enemy, Satan, and how he attacks. We need to keep our eyes open as we go through life, recognizing the minefields, reflecting on the knowledge and wisdom we are obtaining, and building a strong foundation of faith as we study God's Word. It's up to us to choose to do these things. Just as we choose whether to live a happy life or a bitter one. It's all part of the decision to be a student of life or a casualty of it.

Prologue

On July 7, 2020, I woke up and went into my office to study the Word and pray. Instead, I felt the Lord downloading words upon words. I was groggy, sleepy, and not the least bit feeling like writing or being poetic. But the words were coming, and I did not want to lose a single one. I could feel His presence as I tried to capture those words. I quickly picked up a pad of paper and a pen and started writing as fast as I could, trying to keep up. This barrage of words was flowing and spilling over in my mind and out of my pen. I felt like His thoughts were mixing with my experiences on earth, and suddenly, several pages of the pad of paper were full. As I typed it up, I was amazed at the words, the feelings, and the meanings. So softly and tenderly He was comforting me with His thoughts. I believe He was reminding me of His presence every minute of every day.

While I typed this explanation, He filled my mind with more. I believe He was conveying a message to me that I should not fret but realize that things are only temporary. He has overcome the world, and I need to trust Him. In my spirit I know that I am safe in His care. Throughout my life, studying the Bible, I know that I should not fear or fret but stay in prayer and in His presence. He reminds me in so many ways that I am His companion.

Some people still do not believe God conveys things to them, but if they press in and want that kind of companion relationship, He will bless them with it. I know what I know, and one of the things I know is that this sometimes stubborn, sometimes-a-little grouchy-first-thing-in-the-morning person could not even begin to come up with those words. I believe they were inspired by God because they glorify Him. This psalm to me highlights His presence in creation and in my life. They are like a gentle touch—warm and comforting, caring and loving—telling me what I needed to hear during the trying times we were experiencing in the year 2020. They are a gentle reminder of all the things He has made, the very things I love. He dumped His heart into mine and carefully guided my writing. He knows my heart better than anyone on earth, and He knows how to reach me; He often reaches me in this manner. This book is evidence of that. I believe the reason is so that I will share it with others.

Taste and see that the Lord is good; blessed is the one who takes refuge in Him. (Psalm 34:8)

My Companion

Lord, Your greatness and presence are everywhere. They are tangible; I see it in Your creation. I am able to touch, feel, hear, and see Your love in every detail. It is evident in every song the birds sing, the soft fur of an animal, the bright color of every flower and tree. Your presence is in the roar of the ocean and the feast we enjoy from it. Your love for me comes in the sweetness of a piece of fruit or a spoonful of honey from the beehive. How great and wonderful You are, Lord!

I feel Your love and find such joy when I hold a newborn and marvel at the miracle of it all. The mountains, the sky, and the lakes release Your powerful presence to my eyes. Your majesty is everywhere. I feel Your warmth from the sun and Your tears in the rain. I happily take in the breath of Your Spirit in the breeze. Our hearts burst forth with love for those of us who will only acknowledge You.

Your gentle Spirit touches my heart. I release Your presence through my tears, and I am made new. *Companion* is the word that comes to me when I think of You, Lord, because we have a two-way love. You are my constant companion, and I am Yours. I am Your helpmate here on earth, and You are mine in the heavenly realm.

Sometimes You speak to me in a dream; other times You give me one word, like *companion*, but often You call me to a pen and pad. My mind sees a cup overflowing with Your goodness. Your mercies are new every day; I praise You for that, Lord. My mind does not have to dwell in the land of the past because You are my present and my future. You are my refuge from all that will try to destroy me. My trust is only in You, Lord. No other foundation will hold up. No destructive force can override Your presence and Your will. I trust nothing more than You, Lord.

You supply my needs and satisfy the longing of my heart. You push out fear and fill me with hope. I feel Your presence in everything I do, especially when I pray. As companions, we move mountains together. We break strongholds and set the captives free. Together we realign the broken pieces of this world. Together we till the soil and plant the seed for new life to spring forth in the hearts of every man, woman, and child.

Together we are able to restore and heal. Together we are able to do what is necessary for Your presence to come into the places where we go. For You are my constant companion, Lord. You go where I go, Lord, and You rest where I rest.

Please forgive me when I silence Your voice and hide Your presence. Forgive me, Lord, when I forget that You are with me or when I shy away from introductions. This must hurt You deeply.

Lord, may You keep my head in heaven with You while my feet rest here on earth. I ask this so that I can see what You see and feel what You feel. Lord, please help me react as You would in this beautiful but unpredictable place I inhabit for now.

My companion, my Lord. Forgive me once more. Hold my hand so I won't stumble again. Lay out my path before me, and open my eyes to see the course you set me on. May all that is in me praise You, Lord. May all that I am bear witness to Your presence, and may the world see me walking with You, my companion, for the rest of my days, oh, Lord, my rock and my salvation.

A Solid Foundation for Life

When our children were younger, we took them on a vacation through Michigan and into Canada. Along the way, we stopped at the Sleeping Bear Dunes. It was amazing to see that much sand on a lake of all places. We all decided to climb to the top of the dunes so we could see the view. Now, keep in mind, this sand dune is 110 feet tall. This is not a small mound; no, it is a massive mountain of sand! As I was struggling to climb it, I remember thinking, *This is a mistake! I'll never make it to the top because it is just too hard!* It was summer, so it was pretty warm. And every step was *very* difficult because I was sinking deep in sand as I tried to make it up a steep incline. Several times, I had to bend over, use my hands, and practically crawl in order to get to the top. Well, I made it there, and it did have a beautiful view of the lake. But I will not do it again. Once is enough! The whole thing reminded me of how we struggle in life, sometimes similar to sinking in sand because we do not have a solid foundation on which to live our lives.

> They are like a man building a house, who dug down deep and laid the foundation on rock. When a flood came, the torrent struck that house but could not shake it, because it was well built. But the one who hears my words and does not put them into practice is like a man who built a house

on the ground without a foundation. The moment the torrent struck that house, it collapsed and its destruction was complete. (Luke 6:48–49)

A solid foundation, as this Bible verse describes, is like an anchor that keeps us steadfast in a place of safety and peace as the storms of life rage around us. Without any foundation, we collapse and are swept away to face situations and consequences, sometimes many times over, because we lack wisdom, strength, and conviction that can come to us from the Lord.

The song "My Hope Is Built on Nothing Less," by Edward Mote (1934), says it best: "On Christ, the solid Rock I stand; All other ground is sinking sand, all other ground is sinking sand." I love those words because they are so true. What I have learned is that Christ is the only solid foundation we will have in this world. Many things promise stability, but we all know things change, relationships end, the stock market plummets at times, and companies go out of business. So what does a solid foundation established on Christ promise?

Keep your life free from the love of money and be content with what you have, because God has said, "Never will I leave you; never will I forsake you." (Hebrews 13:5)

The things of this world are temporary, but God was there in the beginning and will be there for us in the end. As in the verse above, He promises never to leave us or forsake us. A foundation established in Christ is a place where we can draw all we need in order to stand strong. It is where we receive instruction on how to best live our lives with fewer consequences. A life founded in Christ will open our eyes to all that He has blessed us with so that we can stop, evaluate, and make conscious decisions.

When we come to Christ, we immediately begin to establish a core belief system, meaning we choose to possess a solid, unwavering faith in the Lord and in His Word, the Bible. This builds our solid foundations, but this must come from hearts of love for Him, or we will not do it.

But thanks be to God that, though you used to be slaves to sin, you have come to obey from your heart the pattern of teaching that has now claimed your allegiance. (Romans 6:17)

From this foundation, change begins because the Lord starts to work on us. Right away, we begin to recognize what the people in our lives really mean to us. We begin to give up our selfish ways and to prioritize our relationships over the things of this world. As we begin to spend time with God in prayer, He slows us down, and we are challenged to think about what kind of people we really want to be. We begin to ask ourselves new and different questions, like, "How will my actions hurt or embarrass someone I love?" and, "How will my witness for the Lord be affected if I choose to do this?"

After we decide what kind of people we want to be, we begin to set boundaries for ourselves. I call these boundaries my, "I wills and will nots." In my mind, I resolve beforehand certain things I will not do. Likewise, I also establish in my mind the things I am willing to let go of or do in order to follow Christ. I started this train of thought when I was in elementary school. I remember so clearly thinking, *I will not cheat in school. I will not get in a fight. I will not ever flunk a grade of school.* I did not want to embarrass my parents, whom I loved, and I did not want to embarrass myself or hurt God. The things I would do for God at that age were to pray, ask for forgiveness when I goofed up, and enjoy going to church, Sunday school, Bible school, and church camp.

In Christ, I am also able to realize that I have significance. My character matters to Christ, to myself, and to others. Therefore, every decision I make should be made from a place of awareness and love, drawing on wisdom and strength from the Lord. Read the fifth chapter of Romans.

I know very well how complicated life can be if we live impulsively. It's quicksand out there in the world, so we must be aware and be prepared. Building that foundation will save us an enormous number of consequences and regrets. If we could make good decisions all the time, life would be much easier. I believe that is why God gave us grace through Jesus; He knows life can be very difficult here on earth.

Here are a few things I have learned from bad decisions:

1. When I mess up, I need the Lord's forgiveness and strength right away.
2. I need to ask for forgiveness from the people I hurt and to make amends. Or in other circumstances, I may have to work hard to dig my way out of debt or whatever is needed to rectify the situation.
3. I know I must learn from my mistakes. Even though I have to face the consequences of my poor decisions, God often turns my mistakes into opportunities to help others.
4. I need to recognize how God helps me grow through adversity and be thankful for His work in my life.
5. I must know in my heart that if God has forgiven me, I no longer need to live in shame; shame does not come from God. I must keep my focus on the Lord and trust Him with my future.

Please don't look at your mistakes as hopeless situations. No, think of them as sand dunes you may need to climb. Getting to the top may be hard, but the view at the end of it is beautiful. By asking the Lord for strength, you will be able to resolve to never climb that mound of sand again!

We Are Pottery in Process

I was introduced to pottery in my high school art class. I was hooked the very first time I put my hands to the clay. Yes, there were times I did not get the clay centered on the wheel, and it would all collapse. But oh how I enjoyed the process!

I think of my art class every time I read in the Bible about God being the potter. After having that experience with clay, I began to develop a clearer picture of God as our Creator. Can you imagine having the ability to form the earth, humans, and animals? And I thought it was fun just forming a clay pot!

> Yet you, Lord, are *our Father. We* are the clay, You are the *potter; we* are *all* the *work of* Your hand. (Isaiah 64:8)

We are God's pottery. So, are we just made and that's the end of it, or are we pieces of pottery still in the process of being formed, like unfinished works of art? I think the answer to that question depends on us.

There is always a process in making something usable. Here are the steps for making pottery: Find good clay to work with, prepare the clay, center the clay on the wheel, create a form, remove it from the wheel, let it dry uncovered, let it dry covered, trim and clean the piece, air dry again, fire the piece, glaze it, and fire again. So if we are the clay and God is the potter, how do all these steps relate to us?

First, I believe we have to choose to be moldable, ready and willing to be formed by surrendering ourselves to Christ. As we would not use contaminated clay to make something useful and beautiful, nor should we allow ourselves to remain contaminated by the evil and the negative things of this world. Contamination destroys the vessel.

> Therefore, since we have these promises, dear friends, let us purify ourselves from everything that contaminates body and spirit, perfecting holiness out of reverence for God. (2 Corinthians 7:1)

Second, we have to let the Lord prepare us, work with us, knead, center, and mold us into His plan for our lives. He knows our personalities and gifts; He gave them to us. How willing are we to let go and let God?

> Your hands made me and formed me; give me understanding to learn Your commands. (Psalm 119:73)

Third, we have to be patient as He is patient. It takes time to cure. The drying time cannot be rushed. This step, for some of us, may take many years of testing and learning to grow in our faith to the point where we are moving closer to what we are meant to be.

> But if we hope for what we do not yet have, we wait for it patiently. (Romans 8:25)

Fourth, the hard part, the firing. This process begins to strengthen us so that we cannot be easily broken. At this point, we don't shatter easily when put to the test. We begin to care less about the things of this world that may have mattered to us at one time. We are becoming firmly planted in our faith. The firing usually involves difficult times in our lives that we must work through. It reveals a lot about ourselves. It either makes us stronger or totally defeats us. The outcome depends on whom we put our trust, ourselves or God.

For you, God, tested us; You refined us like silver. (Psalm 66:10)

Fifth and final, the glazing and the last firing. I believe the glazing process comes to us in our mature faith. We may have pushed into God's Word and a relationship with Him so intensely that we became beautiful works of art at a young age. Or, we may have taken our time, learning and maturing over time. All in all, this process depends on what we are willing to put into it. So this step is about our long-established relationship with our Lord and His Holy Spirit, developed by spending time daily with Him. As we do this, we add color to our vessels in the form of our mature spiritual lives, personalities, and presence. The whole process will make us beautiful in God's eyes and gentle and pleasing to others. When we are in the presence of spiritually mature individuals, we find that we love being around them. They display the fruit of the Spirit as in Galatians 5:22–23, and we feel at home in their presence. Their many years of wisdom become valued gifts our hearts and minds are pleased to receive. They are truly earthly treasures of great and lasting value.

Maybe some people think that by the end of their lives, they will not look like a beautiful, glazed vessel of great value. That is correct, but that would only be the outward appearance. So what does God see?

> But the Lord said to Samuel, "Do not consider his appearance or his height, for I have rejected him. The Lord does not look at the things people look at. People look at the outward appearance, but the Lord looks at the heart." (1 Samuel 16:7)

I know that at the end of my parents' lives, their bodies were broken down, and Mom's skin was paper thin. Nevertheless, they were beautiful on the inside. As a daughter, I did not look at them in their physical states as others might have done. I looked at them through eyes of love, just as God does when He looks at us. When we are able to do that, we begin to appreciate the value of each human life. We begin to see each person as God's created and marvelous vessels at every age and form.

Another wonderful aspect of His design is that we are all made for something different. Some for high positions, and some for positions of great importance but less visibility. Each person is very important to God. I believe each life is His divine masterpiece for eternal significance and that He loves us all the same.

> Does not the potter have the right to make out of the same
> lump of clay some pottery for special purposes and some
> for common use? (Romans 9:21)

May we be delighted in whatever vessel we have been given. May we praise God for it because there is no one else exactly like us. We need to remind ourselves everyday that we are masterpieces of God the potter and to treasure His presence in our lives.

> But we have this treasure in jars of clay to show that this
> all-surpassing power is from God and not from us. (2
> Corinthians 4:7)

Effective Bible Study

Very often people start off with good intentions to read the Bible and end up quitting after a short time. There could be several reasons for that, but probably having a busy life would be part of it. I happen to think the biggest reason may be that they just don't get much out of it. It may seem hard for them to understand, or they just lose interest.

One factor that plays heavily into any good intention is the matter of a willing attitude versus a willing spirit. There is a big difference. Being willing to do something, thus having a willing attitude, is an idea that propels us to accomplish our tasks. There are things I don't really enjoy, but I am willing to do them. A willing spirit, on the other hand, is our own decisions to do something with the Holy Spirit's involvement, which means God's involvement in our lives through His Holy Spirit. It is similar to walking in the dark without a flashlight. We can make ourselves do it, but we are uncomfortable because we may stumble. Therefore, we may be less likely to try it again. The flashlight helps us to see and understand the paths we are on, making our journeys pleasant and beneficial.

When we align our spirits with the Lord in this manner, everything changes, especially our desires for Bible study and learning about God and all His attributes. Another thing that changes is the ability to understand what we read and how to apply it to our lives. Why? Because we have invited the author, our Creator, to teach us all things. We are not dependent on our limited capacities and unknowing minds to draw understanding. Yes, there are concordances and other things people have written, and yes, they are good. But what we really want to know is, "What does God want to teach me? What do I need to learn from Him today?"

So the things you will need to embrace an effective Bible study are:

- A willing spirit
- Time set aside several days a week, ideally every day
- A comfortable place to read where you have some quiet private time
- Your Bible
- A journal
- A pen and highlighter
- Prayer
- To clear your mind and meditate on Him and His Word

Besides a willing spirit, we need time. I always enjoyed getting up thirty minutes early and doing my study before I went to work. For one thing, it was very quiet and private during those early hours, and there were no demands on my time. Starting off with Bible reading and prayer changed my whole day. It changed my attitude and blessed my work. On the days I was not able to spend that time in the morning, I could tell a big difference.

When you begin, find a comfortable place to read with correct lighting and the ability to write and read easily. This makes the study more pleasant and something you look forward to.

Find a Bible that you like. There are many translations. My favorites are the NIV and the NLT, but other people may enjoy other versions of the Bible. Explore and find one that speaks to you.

Look for a good writing journal. I like the hardbound ones the best. This is an invaluable tool for writing down scriptures that speak to you. In my book *SOAP How to Clean Up Your Stinking Thinking One Day at a Time,* I write about many subjects using the SOAP method of study. I learned this amazing study method from the book *The Divine Mentor,* by Wayne Cordeiro, and Wayne gave me permission to use it in my first book and in this one.

Basically, S stands for scripture, O stands for observation, A stands for application, and P stands for prayer. This method of Bible study is very powerful and effective. You first write your scripture in your journal (S), and then you record your observation of what that scripture means (O). Next, write how you can apply that scripture to your life (A). Then compose a prayer to God from what you have just learned (P). The journals are powerful testaments to your life and your time in the Word. These journals are wonderful to go back to and read. I would never throw mine away because they represent my sacred time with the Lord.

Don't forget a highlighter. I highlight my Bible and even write in it. I put tabs on certain pages too. I am a serious student of the Lord. After all, B.I.B.L.E. is our *b*asic *i*nstruction *b*efore *l*eaving *e*arth. I do not look at it as a bad thing to highlight a Bible. I look at it as a bad thing to never read the one I have. I might ask, "What would Jesus think?" Does He care about paper and cardboard, or does He care that I learn, put the Holy Scripture in my mind, and return to highlighted places over and over again so that I grow?

Prayer. This is a very important aspect of your study when you invite the Holy Spirit to come join you and teach you all things. Prayer gives you that willing spirit. Of all the things you can do, this one action makes all the difference in your Bible study experience. You are, in essence, giving the Holy Spirit, the very spirit of God, permission to work in you. He is ever so willing to teach you, comfort you, love on you, and help you understand the Word of God. This step will change your life. It will elevate your faith and give you hope and joy like nothing else. The Holy Spirit is the missing link for many believers of the Christian faith. Without the Holy Spirit, we miss out on joy, understanding, and the many gifts God has in store for us. This very thing will possibly decide whether we stay in the faith or wander away from it. To invite the Holy Spirit into my time in the Word, I often pray something like this:

> Holy Spirit come, be with my Bible study today and teach me what you want me to know and show me how to apply it to my life. In Jesus's name, Amen.

> But the Advocate, the Holy Spirit, whom the Father will send in My name, will teach you all things and will remind you of everything I have said to you. (John 14:26)

When studying the Bible, start by praying for the Holy Spirit to come be with you as you open your Bible: Open my eyes that I may see wonderful things in your law (Psalm 119:18). Begin reading, and stop when a verse grabs your attention. At that point, you can use the SOAP method with that verse. I began with the New Testament. I then used *A Year through the Bible* by Tyndale House Publishers. This book has Old Testament, Psalms, Proverbs, and New Testament reading assignments for each day. I think it's much easier than trying to do use the SOAP method on the Old Testament alone.

However you study the Bible, make it work for you. As long as you study God's Word, He will bless you for it.

> You gave your good Spirit to instruct them. You did not withhold your manna from their mouths, and you gave them water for their thirst. (Nehemiah 9:20)

> For the Word of God *is alive and powerful. It is sharper than the sharpest two-edged sword, cutting between soul and spirit, between joint and marrow. It exposes our innermost thoughts and desires.* (Hebrews 4:12 NLT)

> Thy Word is a lamp unto my feet, and a light unto my path. (Psalm 119:105 KJV)

Enjoy the journey!

Reflections of Myself

Reflections Of Myself
I hear the wind, its rumbling roar
Outside my window, one spring more.
Looking forward to new growth
As I am a dear, dear friend.

I lay in darkness as I await deep sleep
And try to clear my mind
Of what I should forget and what I ought to keep.
Tomorrow is coming. What will I do then?
Do I fear what is before me, or take it on the chin?

Day by day, year by year, some of the same old,
some things so dear.

I find I like some things about this place.
I find I hate the weight and wrinkles in my face.
My mind is youthful and caught in no particular time,
But my body is aging and has lost its shine.

I look in the mirror, surprised at what I see;
My mind recalls a different form of me.
I think about what I look like, day in and day out.
I plan to fight it but, I never win the bout!

Aren't we glad that God loves us
Just the way we are?
Oh don't we wish everyone, including ourselves,
Could get that far?

Recycle—Refurbish—Reinvent

I enjoy the shows where they take something old and dirty, clean it up, refurbish it, reinvent it, and make it into something beautiful. I have reclaimed many items over the years. Sometimes things are in good shape, like a lamp I made over. It was black, and I needed an oiled, rubbed, bronze-colored lamp. So I spray-painted it and rubbed just a hint of copper paint on it in various places and bought a new lamp shade. Within a few hours, I had a really nice lamp that fit into my decorating scheme.

It's rewarding to refurbish and reinvent things. There is satisfaction in reclaiming something useful instead of sending it to the landfill. Most of the time, the item can be made into something beautiful. In order for the transformation to take place, a few things have to happen: 1. We have to recognize the value of the item. 2. We have to envision the potential. 3. We have to be willing to put in the time and effort it takes to transform the object.

I think sometimes our lives can be like those objects—in need of a transformation. Years can go by, and we find ourselves in a rut. We look at our lives and find that they are not what we want. I have had both a spiritual drought and a physical crisis when I needed to stop, evaluate, and begin to do things differently. No one else could do it for me. It was my mind and my body; therefore, I had to do it myself.

During my spiritual drought, I began using the SOAP method of studying the Bible. Yes, it took a little time each day, but the rewards were beyond anything I could imagine. I have to say to be spiritually alive and have a close relationship with the Lord on a daily basis is phenomenal. The result of that decision is my book *SOAP How to Clean Up Your Stinking Thinking One Day at a Time.* I had no way of knowing where the decision to get into the Bible and spend time with God would take me. What a wonderful experience!

My second issue was my health. I had doctors tell me they didn't know what else to do for me. At that point, I knew I had to make a choice: put up with the issues, or do something about them. Like most people, I put up with the issues for several years, until I could no longer. I believed God heals, but I also knew I needed to do my part. I began to get away from foods that were harmful and started to eat natural food, nothing processed. I got off sugars and most grains and dairy. I found out what other foods were bothering me and eliminated them. I began to eat and drink 100 percent healthfully. Yes, it was hard, but most things worthwhile are. It's amazing that when I began to let go and let God, my life got so much better.

To sum up the process of recycling my life, I go back to those three steps with scripture.

> First, I had to recognize that I am of great worth: "Rather, it should be that of your inner self, the unfading beauty of a gentle and quiet spirit, which is of great worth in God's sight" (1 Peter 3:4).

> Second, I had to envision my possibilities by standing on God's promise: "I can do all things through Christ who strengthens me" (Philippians 4:13 NKJV). If I could not find this strength, then I would not be able to believe in the possibility of a better life.

> Third, I had to be willing to do the hard work and change the way I was thinking in order to obtain something better for myself. Hard work resulted in change, but all the years

of talk got me nowhere: "All hard work brings a profit, but mere talk leads only to poverty" (Proverbs 14:23). Prayer and staying in the Bible gave me great strength.

There have been many times in my life when I have had to go back and work through those steps again. It's pretty easy to get sidetracked and begin to get down on ourselves. What we need to remember is that we are precious to God, and He has not given up on us; we have simply given up on ourselves. Sometimes, too, we find ourselves believing the lies of others or of Satan. We must go back to the scriptures, read what God says about us, and ignore everything else. It's a good thing to verbally or mentally reject the lies, saying, "I reject this in the name of Jesus!" Then begin to speak the things in scripture that God says.

It is God who arms me with strength and keeps my way secure. (Psalm 18:32)

Do not fear, for I have redeemed you; I have summoned you by name; you are mine. (Isaiah 43:1b)

"For I know the plans I have for you," declares the Lord, "plans to prosper you and not to harm you, plans to give you hope and a future." (Jeremiah 29:11)

When we believe those lies that cripple us, we are broken and unusable by God for a time. We are in need of repairs. We must pray and ask the Creator to begin to fix what is broken in our spirits and to bind up any spirit of doubt, fear, and confusion. Everything needs some repair every now and again.

But now in Christ Jesus you who once were far away have been brought near by the blood of Christ. For He Himself is our peace. (Ephesians 2:13–14a)

The Lord is close to the brokenhearted and saves those who are crushed in spirit. The righteous person may have

many troubles, but the Lord delivers him from them all.
(Psalm 34:18–19)

He heals the broken hearted and binds up their wounds.
(Psalm 147:3)

Whether starting to read the Bible, working on our health, or something else that we need to tackle, it will always start out hard because we have to die to our own stubborn wills first. Little by little, it will get easier, and then we will begin to see the changes. The key to success is to allow God to help and guide us. There is great power in combining our lives with the Lord's.

But those who hope in the Lord will renew their strength.
They will soar on wings like eagles; they will run and not
grow weary, they will walk and not be faint. (Isaiah 40:31)

It is a wonderful and worthwhile endeavor to rescue things from destruction, especially if they are our lives.

All That I Am

I love reading the Bible, and quite often certain words in a verse grab me like Velcro and won't let go! Of course, there are always other things calling for my attention, but sometimes those verses keep coming to my mind. They propel me to dig deeper and find out what the Lord is trying to communicate to me. I love that supernatural character of God at work through His Word, speaking to me through His Holy Spirit. I liken it to the Lord, handing me my lunch money for the day. But not just enough money for a so-so lunch. No, it's a lot of money for a tasty, super-nutritious lunch that fills me up and lasts all day! Manna from heaven, I call it. In order to get the lunch, I have to go to where it is being served—the Bible. In order for the manna from heaven to give me the nutrition, I have to digest it; I have to read and study God's Word.

On one such occasion, these verses from the book of Psalms just happened to grab me, and I knew the Lord had something rich and meaningful to teach me. Finding treasures in God's Word is always a joy.

> Let all that I am praise the Lord; with my whole heart, I *will* praise *his holy name.* (Psalm 103:1 NLT)

Now, Psalms 103:1, 22; 104:1, 35; and 146:1 from the NLT version all say, "Let all that I am praise the Lord." I looked it up in other versions of the Bible, but I have to say the way it is written in the NLT version spoke to me. These words made me ask myself, "Who am I, and how do all these things that I am praise the Lord?"

Seriously, how often do we take the time to sit back and think about ourselves in that context? This is deep, so let me explain what these verses mean to me. I'll start with myself and, "Who am I?" I am a daughter of the Most High God, a daughter to my parents, a sister, wife, mother, sister-in-law, grandmother, friend. Now, "What am I?" I'm kind, compassionate, loving, caring (or at least try hard to be), a prayer warrior, an artist, a writer, cook, gardener, housekeeper, not to mention all the job titles I've had in my life.

To me, who I am is where life has taken me. These are titles that came to me through birth and relationships. These are the names that are dear to me. They are essentially who I am inside my mind, spirit, and in the heavenly and earthly realms, like mom, grandma, daughter, wife, and friend.

What I am are those things that I made a choice to be. Even though God may have given me those abilities, I still choose to accept and use them. I choose to be kind and loving. I choose to be a writer and an artist. I chose to have the type of jobs I held. What I am can change quickly by choice or by not following the Lord. For example, I can choose not to be nice, or I can choose to quit a career or hobby. But who I am will always be the same, even though the people with whom I am in a relationship may leave me in death.

Another thing to consider is that God makes all of us unique, with different strengths and weaknesses, so that plays a factor in all that I am as well. That means my worship will be different from another person's. It will be unique and treasured by God. All our praises together would be like all the different voices in a choir. Each voice is different, but when we all come together in admiration for our Lord, there is perfection.

To take all that I am and praise the Lord would mean that I use what I am and who I am with every opportunity I have been given to glorify the Lord. As believers, we have to desire to please and praise the Lord so much that our minds are fixed on Him every day of our lives. So what would that look like?

As we live out our lives, we have the ability to affect others in a positive way. For example, as a mother, I was able to teach my children about God and how to be polite, loving, and kind. As a wife, friend, or Christian, I am able to show respect for others and to demonstrate love and forgiveness, pray for and with others, and maybe come to their aid when needed. In every little part of my world, I have the ability to praise God by taking care of what He loves, His people and His creation. So I am saying that we are not only able to praise the Lord with our voices, as we have always known, but also in service and the giving of our time, energy, and love. In this way, every part of our bodies praises the Lord—our mouths, limbs, brains, hearts, spirits. Everything. All that I am!

> The King will reply, "Truly I tell you, whatever you did
> for one of the least of these brothers and sisters of mine,
> you did for me." (Matthew 25:40)

By praising the Lord through our actions, we develop intentional, deeper walks with the Lord, and He is so good to bless us for it. What I have noticed in people who live this way is that they have their minds engaged.

They must intentionally say to themselves, "I'm not doing this out of selfish ambition. I'm doing this for the Lord! I demonstrate my love for Him because He first loved me." When we can refocus our lives toward a purpose like that, then the purpose becomes the means by which we become more sincere people. Our compassion and hard work are viewed as honest acts of love, not acts for reward or show. This is very refreshing and comforting. It is a gift to be friends or family members with these devoted saints of God.

Genuine people are truly loved, admired, and blessed spiritually. This is something we must decide in our own minds to be important to us. This priority comes from a relationship with Jesus Christ. Without that, none of this will make sense or even be important. This relationship calls us into a vibrant way of living. It is a higher calling to a higher standard of behavior, compassion, and a desire to achieve a higher level of excellence in our work because we are working not just for ourselves but for the Lord. It is all because we truly want to, not because we are made to. That's what a life with Christ is all about—freedom, the choice to be loved unconditionally by God and to love Him in return.

Other ways we can praise God are with our voices in song and in prayer. We praise Him from the longings of our hearts, our desires to be with Him in communication and in His Word. We praise God through our weaknesses by giving them to Him in prayer and asking for His strength. Don't we love it when our children or friends ask us for help because they need our presence and our strength? They may need the skills that we possess. It praises us that they recognized our abilities and acknowledged our worth and friendship. Isn't that how God is also praised?

> But He said to me, "My grace is sufficient for you, for My power is made perfect in weakness." Therefore I will boast all the more gladly about my weaknesses, so that Christ's power may rest on Me. (2 Corinthians 12:9)

Praising God with all that I am is about being able to lay it all out there before Him, being honest, sincere, thankful, and humble. Taking everything we have been given and presenting it at the feet of Jesus. Our gifts, our weaknesses, who we are, what we are, and even what we long to be. We are saying to God by our vulnerabilities, "I accept You, I cherish Your love, and I trust You completely with all that I am and long to be." Now that is praise!

Understanding Anger

I am frequently amazed that no matter how many times I read through the Bible, certain verses will catch my attention at a particular time and reveal their meanings when I actually need them the most. I find myself thinking, *Why did I not catch that before?* It is the mystery of God and how He works through His words to speak to us. That's why we say it's the living Word of God, as in Hebrews 4:12.

I found all this to be true about Matthew 5:21–22 (NLT), which says,

> You have heard that our ancestors were told, You must not murder. If you commit murder, you are subject to judgment, but I say, if you are even angry with someone, you are subject to judgment! If you call someone an idiot, you are in danger of being brought before the court. And if you curse someone, you are in danger of the fires of hell.

I may have been a bit confused by this before because I remember the story of Jesus getting angry in the temple and turning over the money changers' tables. Now I understand that He is God, and I am not! What I mean is that God has the ability to handle anger; I do not. True anger can be an extremely toxic emotion that can overtake one's whole being, pushing out love. It has the ability to overcome the positive and good aspects of our spirits, our personalities, and our actions. For these reasons, even when someone hurts me or when I see injustice in the world, I may be upset, but I cannot let it turn into anger.

We are going to have emotional responses about the bad things that happen. We are emotional beings. But being upset about something and letting it turn into anger has to be a choice. I don't think many of us see it as that. We often feel justified because we were wronged. That's right; we are hurt, and we feel anger. But are we to hold on to it? It would be like holding on to a live electric wire. Something very bad is going to go through one's whole body and do a lot of damage. That is what unchecked anger does. It turns to bitterness and hatred and starts to destroy us from the inside out, harming us mentally, physically, and spiritually, moving us away from any kind of peaceful existence.

> Refrain from anger and turn from wrath; do not fret—it leads only to evil. (Psalm 37:8 NIV)

> Stop being angry! Do not lose your temper-it only leads to harm. (Psalm 37:8 NLT)

One very helpful thing to do is to remove ourselves, if possible, from the constant source that causes the reaction of anger in us. There are many things in this world that can cause us to be angry. It could be the news. Turn it off. Find another avenue, like a website or newspaper or app on your phone, to get your news. In this way, you are only reading as much as you need in order to pray and stay informed. Daily exposure to negative things will develop into anger. There are often people in our lives who upset us. Are they people we could distance ourselves from? Maybe it's something at work or home. But the secret to living in this world is to take things and filter them through God.

In our world we hear, read, and see many things. We immediately decide whether to accept or reject these things. Without thinking, we file this information away in our brains. If we keep it, it can do two things—motivate us or hurt us. This depends on how we understand that information, and how we decided to react to it. When we filter those things through God in prayer and by reading and understanding His scripture, we are given a clearer picture of how we are to use this information. Let me use an example to help you understand my point.

Human trafficking sets off all kinds of emotions in me. If I let it take over my thoughts for too long, I become very angry about it. Then the anger begins to destroy my sense of well-being, my joy, my ability to be thankful and happy, and my very ability to sleep at night. But when I only let it upset me and take those emotions to God in prayer, I release to Him those feelings, and I know that I have battled that horrible injustice in prayer.

We cannot stand in anger because it creates a disconnect in our communications with God. Anger is a sin, and God cannot be in sin with us. He still loves us, but the close communication is broken until we repent; we must ask Him to forgive us and help us through it.

> In your anger do not sin. Do not let the sun go down while you are still angry, and do not give the devil a foothold. (Ephesians 4:26–27)

> Get rid of all bitterness, rage and anger, brawling and slander, along with every form of malice. (Ephesians 4:31)

Why should we care if our anger does not produce in us what God desires? If we say we believe but do not care about what God thinks, do we really believe? Do we really love and respect God, or is it just lip service? If we are truly committed to God, we will believe what the Bible says, and we will be concerned with what God cares about—believers and nonbelievers alike. We are here to show nonbelievers something different, something other than anger and hate. We are to display love and forgiveness and the path to eternal life through Jesus Christ.

> Because human anger does not produce the righteousness that God desires. (James 1:20)

We need to soak our minds in what is good and honorable. We need to have many positive influences in our lives, including scripture, praise music, the wonderful fellowship of positive people, as well as close communication with the Holy Spirit daily. This is how I survive. Think of it like a light switch. When anger comes on us, we are in the dark, so we must choose to intentionally flip the switch. Turn on the light by taking it to God. Let us meditate on and live out Philippians 4:8: "Finally, brothers and sisters, whatever is true, whatever is noble, whatever is right, whatever is pure, whatever is lovely, whatever is admirable—if anything is excellent or praiseworthy—think about such things."

This is key: We all mess up. I thank God He forgives. We have to remember to offer grace to others just as we want them to offer grace to us when we slip up. Everyone goes through pain and heartache, which at times will cause us to be unfriendly and maybe even rude. We must not take offense. We must pray and forgive. We can all learn to be patient with our fellow travelers because no one escapes the trials and tribulations of life on this earth.

> A person's wisdom yields patience; it is to one's glory to overlook an offense. (Proverbs 19:11 NIV)

> Sensible people control their temper; they earn respect by overlooking wrongs. (Proverbs 19:11 NLT)

Fear, Lies, and Jail Cells

In many situations, we find that there is no stronger, more debilitating emotion than fear. Unchecked, fear knocks a person down and drags him or her off into a state of confinement for as long as it takes to distrust the lie that began it all.

> Of all the liars in the world, sometimes the worst are our own fears. (Rudyard Kipling)

The Invisible Jail Cell

A Fictional Short Story

I remember that day. It burned into my mind. It hurt me for many years, like a wound that would not heal. The embarrassment, the comments, the looks on those kids' faces lay there in that open wound. It was the lie I relived over and over every time I was asked to step out and try something new. It was the lie that kept me in an invisible jail cell.

I was an only child, born to two very intelligent professional people who loved me but were not aware of me. I know that doesn't make sense, but what I mean is that they were aware of my presence but not of my mental and spiritual needs. They were wrapped up in their professions and in themselves. If I needed to get anywhere or buy anything, they were on it. They saw that I had plenty of food and a nice place to live, but did they ever ask me what I felt or what I was thinking? Never! Oh, they were concerned with my grades and activities, and they made sure I had a cake and presents on my birthday and at Christmas. But that was about it. Having no siblings to talk to, my life felt very lonely.

My parents named me Betsy, after a great-aunt whom I never knew. I disliked it because it was considered an old-fashioned name, easy to make fun of. On top of that, I had to wear glasses. I always enjoyed schoolwork and got very good grades. I had nice enough clothes, but I was modest and quiet. In school, all those things got you labeled a nerd. As it happened, I was drawn to other smart people like myself. It was funny how some of them were bothered by what the so-called normal kids said, and others simply laughed it off.

I always got along with my teachers because they loved the kids who would actually do their homework and behave in class. I'm sure to them it was like finding a pot of gold. Mrs. Rose was my eighth-grade English teacher. On one particular spring afternoon, she handed our class a writing assignment and gave us a deadline of one week for its completion. Well, that was easy enough for me, so I sat out researching my subject and writing about it. On the day it was due, Mrs. Rose announced to the class that we would take turns reading our reports in front of the class. Now, she had never asked that of us before, so I was taken by surprise. Sitting there, I was filled with dread, waiting for my turn in front of the class. I was quiet and shy and had no experience talking in front of any group of people, least of all a class full of people who treated me like an outcast. When I got up to read my report, I could not get the words to come out right and made a mess of the whole thing. I embarrassed myself and gave the class a lot to laugh and comment about. I will never forget their laughter and their jokes at my expense. That day changed something in me that lasted for a long time.

By the time I entered college, I had begun using my middle name, Ann. I got contacts and tried to change some things about myself, but I was still shy. At that age, most people were less concerned about who I was and more about who they were. I could fly under the radar and not be noticed, and that was fine by me! I still had a debilitating fear of public speaking, and I would avoid any kind of activity that put me in the limelight or drew attention to me. My self-esteem in social areas after that day in middle school was pretty low. I knew one reason was because I had no one at home who would listen and care, so I held it all in for years.

After college, I started a good job. I was very happy with my skills but not my lingering fears. Those fears were like a ball and chain around my ankle. I really liked the company I was working for and met some very nice people. One lady in particular grabbed my attention. She was different. I couldn't put my finger on it, but I knew I wanted some of the confidence and joy that she had. We began eating lunch together and got to know each other better. Eventually, I felt I was able to trust her, but I still wasn't sure I could open up to her about my fears.

After being with the company for a time, my boss approached me and told me it was time for me to begin conducting some of the weekly business meetings. I was petrified, unable to say a word. There was no place to run. I knew I couldn't quit my job and wondered how I was going to make it through these meetings every week.

My new friend, Sandy, saw my face and asked me what was wrong. I finally told her of my paralyzing fear. It was a Friday afternoon, and she said, "I know just what you need. Will you come to church with me on Sunday?" I didn't know what to say. I had not been in a church for anything other than a wedding or a funeral. It just wasn't anything that was important to my parents, so it never became important to me. But I was distraught and ready to try anything.

Sandy and I met for dinner Saturday night, and she briefly told me about her church and what to expect. She talked about how friendly and loving all the people there were. She also told me something else that surprised me. She said that she, too, had a few bouts with fear and that what she learned while attending church helped her through it. I was amazed! I never would have guessed that to be the case with Sandy. She was kind and smart and handled everything at work with confidence and poise. Well, she didn't say much more about herself that night, but she had succeeded in helping me to feel more at ease for Sunday morning.

Sunday came. I met Sandy in the church parking lot, and we walked in together. It was a nice church, comfortably decorated, seating around three hundred or so, and the people were very friendly. We found our seats, and the music started. I was immediately drawn to the music. I didn't know why, but it was like being hungry for something I didn't even know that I liked. As luck would have it, the pastor was starting a series about fear. The coincidence of it all got my attention. He began by reading 2 Timothy 1:7 that I will never forget: "For God has not given us a spirit of fear and timidity, but of power, love and self-discipline."

By then, I was eager to hear more. He went on to talk about how God is love and how perfect love casts out fear. It felt like he was talking directly to me. All the things he was saying were what I had been living. He called fear a lie and said Satan was the perpetrator of the lie. He explained that Satan wants to put us in an emotional tomb and roll the biggest, heaviest stone in the doorway to our futures and our abilities to do great things. The pastor went on to say that the tomb could not keep Jesus from His mission, and because of Jesus, we cannot be kept in the tomb either! He told us that it was time to nail the lies to the cross and start a new life in the presence of the only one who can break those chains and release us from Satan's hold on our lives: Jesus Christ. A lightning bolt of truth! What is it that they say? "And the truth shall set you free!" That day I went forward and gave my life to Christ. I didn't have to think about it. I was drawn to the life Jesus had to offer, and I have never looked back.

The truth of the Bible, those precious words, began to sweep away the lies that bound me. The lies that I was not good enough, pretty enough, capable, interesting, or valuable. All those lies for all those years had led to an overwhelming fear in so many areas of my life, crippling me and keeping me from so many good things.

I know now that we naturally believe lies when we are never given the truth. I made a pact with God that if I ever was blessed with children, I would be there for them mentally, physically, and most important, spiritually. If Sandy had not cared enough for me to ask me to church to hear the truth, those lies and fears would have cost me my job and any opportunity for an abundant and fulfilling life.

I thank Jesus every day for freedom. I thank Him every day for opportunities to step out in faith and to let the light shine in the darkness for all those innocent victims of invisible jail cells. Freedom in Christ: There is nothing like it! Praise God I found it! Praise God for Sandy and for the day the Lord arranged a sermon for one very lost person who came from a world without compassion and love. What I realize all these years later about the kids who laughed off the ridicule is that they had parents who told them the truth in love. They were parents who communicated with their children and put a higher priority on their spiritual and mental lives than on anything else. I now see that the world does not understand that true freedom and happiness come through the precious death and resurrection of Jesus Christ.

I have to say, my love for Christian music has been my rock through it all. I especially love the song "Fear Is a Liar," by Zack Williams. All in all, I am totally convinced of one amazing truth: Perfect love casts out fear, and perfect love comes only from the Father, Son, and Holy Spirit.

> Even though I walk through the darkest valley, I will fear *no evil, for you are with* me; your rod and your staff, they comfort me. (Psalm 23:4 NIV)

> Lord, even when your path takes me through the valley of deepest darkness, fear will never conquer me, for you already have! Your authority is my strength and my peace. The comfort of your love takes away my fear. I'll never be lonely, for you are near. (Psalm 23:4 TPT)

> Have I not commanded you? Be strong and courageous. Do not be afraid; do not be discouraged, for the Lord your God will be with you wherever you go. (Joshua 1:9)

Walking in the Truth, Led by the Spirit of God

I love it when God teaches me an important life lesson in a funny and unforgettable way through my experiences. Often, those lessons come through hard and difficult times, but once in a while, they are just funny, treasured moments. One such lesson came to me at the grocery store of all places.

Our local grocery has a sale once a week in which all their produce is half price. My husband and I go from time to time and take advantage of it. On this particular day, while we were shopping, I had my attention on some lettuce in the cooler when I heard a man behind me say, "We should have gotten a bigger cart!" Well, I thought, *What? There are no bigger carts!* This store does not have those smaller half-size carts, so I wondered, *Are they buying a lot just because it's on sale?* I had pictured a regular-size cart overflowing with produce. I was thinking about how people go nuts when things are on sale and buy too much. See, I know something about this because as much as I hate to admit it, I have done the same thing if it's something I use all the time. So I turned around thinking I already knew what I was going to see. But what I actually saw was a little girl around six years old trying to push one of those really small grocery carts for children, which was full of fruits and vegetables. Of course those carts hold hardly anything, so it was overflowing. Her parents were picking up the things that had fallen out. I laughed at the sight, and they laughed too.

It was a gentle reminder to me that no, I don't know it all! I may think I know what is going on by what I hear, but in reality, only God knows what's going on in someone's life. It reminded me of the song "God Only Knows," by For King and Country. That song really hit home with me the first time I heard it. It made me think about the many times I, too, felt only God knew what I was going through. There were times in my life that were so difficult that I could not put into words what I was feeling. And maybe in reality, I just didn't want to express them.

Knowing the things that I have been through, I find it so easy to get caught up in other people's lives. Sometimes that is good, and sometimes it is not. It is not good when we hear things through the grapevine about people and for some reason, we buy into believing what we hear. Just like I did by hearing that man speak and not seeing with my eyes the true situation. Before we know it, our minds have made up what we start to believe as the truth. When we think about that logically, it's just plain ridiculous.

I have found the best thing to do when I hear something is to pray about it first, and if God wants me to go to that person and find out the truth, the opportunity to do so will open. At that point, we must pray for wisdom and guidance to know what to say and to guard our minds and our mouths. This takes a concerted effort, and I have to admit I have not always been good at this. But as a student, I'm learning. Praise God for His grace!

> Those who trust in themselves are fools, but those who walk in wisdom are kept safe. (Proverbs 28:26)

Have you ever been on the receiving end of someone's opinion when that person really has no idea what he or she is talking about? It can be frustrating and hurtful. Oh, if we could just remember what that felt like before we do it to others, wouldn't that change our behaviors?

I may refer to this off and on, but it's vitally important: We are so easily pulled away from what is good and right. In order to stay in the circumference of Galatians 5:22—which is love, joy, peace, forbearance, kindness, goodness, faithfulness, gentleness, and self-control—we need to be in the Word of God, the Bible, every day. Every day. I'm not kidding, every day! I know this to be true because I have experienced the weakness that comes a day or two after being away from time with the Lord. Then when even more days go by without this time, I find it easier to revert to my old behavior or pick up something new. The Lord is my only strength; through daily prayer and Bible study, I am able to live better and be stronger. There is so much untruth and bad behavior all around us. It is very easy to be influenced if we are not on guard.

God is our protection. When we get out of His presence, we are vulnerable. Open your eyes to the fact that you know how easy it is for a confessed Christian to slip and fall. Don't be judgmental; it can happen to any of us. The weather outside God's presence is freezing rain, and some may know how to ice-skate on it for a while and not fall, but most of us fall right away. Sadly, the whole world—Christians and non-Christians alike—are waiting to catch our latest performance and judge us.

Truth, isn't that a beautiful thing? Only by living in God's presence by the Holy Spirit will we know the truth and recognize the lies.

> But when He, the Spirit of truth, comes, He will guide you into all the truth. He will not speak on His own; He will speak only what He hears, and He will tell you what is yet to come. (John 16:13)

The Gift of Compassion

Compassionate love seeks to heal and restore those in need. It knows no age, race, or fault. It is the pure love given to us from our Creator to share with the human race in abundance and with grace.

> Because of the Lord's great love we are not consumed, for his compassions never fail. They are new every morning; great is your faithfulness. (Lamentations 3:22)

Abundant Love

A Fictional Short Story

My name is Dawn. I am now in my sixties. I am recounting my life by writing down my story. It's funny how the years go by, and I rarely take the time to look back and see all the twists and turns that brought me to where I am today. I can now see how God directed people in and out of my life for His purpose and glory.

I was born to a young unwed mother, and I never knew who my father was. I didn't even know if I had an extended family. My mother ran away from whatever was in her past and never talked about it. Of course, I was a child and not able to understand much about it anyway. When I was four, my mother died, and I was taken away and put in a foster home. I had no idea what was happening or what actually happened to my mother. As a little child, people just take you and tell you very little, and there is nothing you can do about it. My first foster home wasn't too bad, but I grieved my mother, and I was very confused.

Those people had to move out of state, so I was put in another foster home when I was five. It was not a good place. The foster father was very unkind to me, but he treated his own children better. My foster mother basically followed whatever her husband did. About that time, I started kindergarten, and I really liked my teacher, Mrs. Harp. She was always very kind and patient with me. I had a lot to learn since I did not have someone at home who would teach me things.

By the end of the school year, my foster dad was getting pretty abusive. Mrs. Harp could see a change in me. On one particular day, she saw bruises on my upper arm and called in the school counselor. Children's services came, talked to my teacher, and gave her some of my history. She was very distraught as they moved me to yet another foster home.

Mrs. Harp could not have children because of an abortion she had as a teen. As she told me later, she was once married to a wonderful man who had taught her the love and forgiveness of Jesus Christ. They decided that when they were ready, they would adopt children. She understood me so much better because she suffered, too, because she had lost her one true love, her rock, her husband of five years. He was killed by a drunk driver two years before I started school. When she found out my history, her heart broke for me, and she set about working with children's services to become a foster parent for me and perhaps even to adopt me.

I'll never forget that life-changing day. A lady from children's services came to get me and told me I was going to another foster home. I felt hopeless and helpless. I was very afraid of what I might face only to be taken to my precious Mrs. Harp! She showed me love and acceptance and taught me the things her husband had taught her. Together we grew in our faith and in the loving fellowship of other believers at her husband's church. We were two people who never grew up knowing God, so we studied the Bible and deepened our understanding of His Word together. Oh, what wonderful memories we made.

When I was ten, my mother, Mrs. Harp, married a pastor who had lost his wife to cancer. He had a boy and a girl, who became my brother and sister. Together we made a family out of the broken pieces of our lives. Over time, those pieces became glued together with God's love. My mother and this new family made me who I am today. They gave me the tools I needed to face the world, love people, and show the compassion that I had been shown.

After attending school to become a nurse, I rented a little house in the suburbs of the city. I moved in next to an older lady raising her grandson, James. She told me she was raising him because her daughter had died from a drug overdose, and the little boy's father was serving several years in prison. It was a sad and complicated situation. This little boy was a sweet child but full of energy. It was almost too much to manage for his elderly grandmother. Because I was a nurse, and they didn't have much money, I would help my neighbor out when James got hurt or was ill. I began to get pretty attached to them, and I would take James out to the park and other places to give his grandmother a break. She was a wonderful lady who became a dear friend. This special relationship went on for a few years, until one day James's grandmother got very ill and passed. There was no place for James to go.

I immediately sought custody of him and was very surprised to find out that his grandmother had left me her house and the money from her life insurance to raise James and see that he got an education. So here I was, raising a boy as my own son, doing exactly what Mrs. Harp had done for me. All because, like Mrs. Harp, I was in the right place at the right time and willing to show love that I had received.

James grew up, went to school, married, and later opened a place for the youth in our community. He always said there was a need for a place for children to go after school to get them off the streets and away from the drugs that took his parents.

I did not marry. I could not find someone who was right for James and me. I volunteered at the free clinic a few days a month while also working my full-time job at the local hospital. Later, I also became a volunteer with the Big Sisters of America program, working with girls from around the area who needed a friend and mentor. James and I faithfully attended church, and he became involved with the youth ministries there. My life was full with James and my adopted family.

I often think about how my life could have turned out differently. I have truly been blessed. What I now know is that we are rescued by God to, in turn, rescue others. Sometimes we are called to do this with prayer and friendship, and sometimes with provisions, but always with love. We are all called to live out compassionate love, God's love, to those in need. I remember asking, "Lord, how many people can I actually love?" Immediately in my mind, I knew He would make it possible for me to love as many as He sent my way, and I would not have to worry. All we need is to be willing and available. God will do the rest.

> Therefore, as God's chosen people, holy and dearly loved,
> clothe yourselves with compassion, kindness, humility,
> gentleness and patience. (Colossians 3:12)

An Instrument of Your Peace

I think most of us would love to find a peaceful place where we can get away from all the turmoil and chaos we see in our world. Sometimes we can't wait to get home and shut out everything, even if it's just for a few hours. But our homes are often not peaceful either. We may find that what we really need is to just be around a peaceful person. It is a true gift to actually find someone who listens to us, shows concern and unconditional love. It's like finding a fountain of cool, refreshing water when we are hot, dry, and thirsty. It refreshes us, replenishes our spirits, and calms our fears.

I remember my grandmother and my mother having that spirit. It was such a comforting thing to be around them. You almost felt like you were wrapped up in a fuzzy, soft blanket on a cold winter day when you were in their presence. I only grew up with one grandparent, and she was very special. I remember going to her house and enjoying her warm welcome and her homemade molasses cookies. She was always so calm and cheerful and made me feel so loved. Oh, how I cherished the time I spent with her. All I have now are memories of the both of them and the wonderful times we had. But do you know what? All the years we shared served to make me want to be just like them. By being in their presence, I was being mentored and taught a view of how life can be when we live under the influence of a loving Savior.

We are teachers whether we know it or not. We are either teachers of peace and calmness or of chaos and stress, of love and relationship or of hate and disharmony. Have we ever stopped to think what kind of people we really want to be and what we want our lives to portray to others?

The words, "an instrument of your peace," came to me when I was going about my day, not thinking about what I was going to write. That happens often, and I needed to quickly write down the words before I forgot them. I set about looking up the word *instrument* to get a clearer picture of what it means in that sentence. An instrument can be a tool used in science, a thing used in pursuing a goal or policy, something used in measuring, or used in making music.

In the Bible, mostly in the KJV, the word *instrument* was used several ways. In 1 Chronicles12:33 (KJ21), it talks about "instruments of war." Romans 6:13 (KJV) tells us, "Neither yield ye your members as instruments of unrighteousness unto sin, but yield yourselves unto God as those that are alive from the dead, and your member as instrument of righteousness" unto God. And Isaiah 38:20 (NIV) reads "The Lord will save me and will sing with stringed instruments all the days of our lives in the temple of the Lord."

In all these applications, an instrument is something to be used for a purpose. Did you get that? Used for a purpose! We are here, born in this time frame, not another, for a purpose. God gave us special gifts and abilities for such a time as this. Our goals should be to find them and use them to serve the Lord.

> From one man He made all the nations, that they should inhabit the whole earth; and He marked out their appointed times in history and the boundaries of their lands. (Acts 17:26)

We are uniquely made to accomplish certain things. But ultimately, we are all called to the same thing: to be instruments of peace, displaying all these attributes of Christ to a dark and dismal, chaotic world.

I have always loved this beautifully worded prayer known as "An Instrument of Your Peace." It is a prayer of Saint Francis of Assisi, who died in 1226. It is so remarkable to me that something around eight hundred years old lives on and became a favorite prayer of mine. This prayer says it all, and I feel it is divinely inspired.

Just a little background on this prayer. There are different written versions. Though similar, many leave out the line, "where there is discord, union." I have no idea why. I have always loved that line and feel it is very important. Is that not part of one's purpose here on earth? I found the version I like at bootsandbible. info and believe to be more factual:

> Lord, make me an instrument of your peace;
> where there is hatred, let me sow love;
> where there is injury, pardon;
> where there is discord, union;
> where there is doubt, faith;
> where there is despair, hope;
> where there is darkness, light;
> and where there is sadness, joy.

O Divine Master, grant that I may not so much seek to be consoled, as to console; to be understood, as to understand; to be loved, as to love; for it is in giving that we receive, it is in pardoning that we are pardoned, and it is in dying that we are born to eternal life. Amen.
—Saint Francis of Assisi

Oh, to be around people who live out that prayer. Just to be in their presence is like heaven on earth. It is a goal of mine to be like that. How about you? We all need goals, things to strive for. Who says our goals have to be something just for us? Why can't they be goals that benefit everyone?

Oh, Lord, help me be the cool drink a thirsty soul needs, the calming ear that listens, and the vessel that shows Your love. Help me, Lord, be an instrument of Your peace. Amen.

> Love and faithfulness meet together; righteousness and
> peace kiss each other. (Psalm 85:10)

Philippians 4:13
Sally's Favorite Bible Verse

I can do all things through Christ

who gives me strength.

Philippians 4:13 (NKJV)

Where Is True Happiness?
A Fictional Short Story

Shannon sat in her new apartment in disbelief that her college graduation was already over. She knew she had several days to relax before she started her new job. Even though she was excited about this new chapter of her life, Shannon felt empty and unhappy. After the ceremony and the parties, the friends she made over the last four years, like she, had moved on. Even though they all said they would keep in touch, she knew that was highly unlikely. When she looked back at her high school friends, she really only had one or two with whom she maintained any form of communication, so she knew how it went. Now here she sat, all alone, contemplating her past and her future as she said to herself, "Somehow I feel it's all meaningless."

At one time, she thought school sports, friends, and parties would make her happy. And yes, she did have some fun, but it never lasted. Shannon thought a boyfriend would fill the void, but very soon she became pretty critical of him and stopped dating him. She remembered looking forward to college so she could begin her life as an adult. Even though Shannon had some good times in college, she knew she was embracing a fake form of happiness. She again voiced her thoughts aloud: "Everything has left me empty. Why? Does a person have to use alcohol or drugs to find happiness? Where can I find true happiness?"

Shannon didn't want to talk to someone her own age about serious stuff. She had found no comfort in that over the years. Maybe it was because she really didn't have a true friend, meaning one who really cared for someone else a little more than himself or herself. She didn't think she wanted to talk to some strange pastor or counselor, and she knew she couldn't talk to her mom. She wondered, *Mom has not known happiness since my father left us, so how could she begin to help me?*

Out of all the people she knew, there was only one person who would have the answers, Grandma. She laughed as she thought that her grandmother could go through a hurricane, lose everything, and still keep smiling. Her grandfather had passed a while back, and her grandmother was sad but still kept going on in the same manner that Shannon had come to love. As she was sitting there contemplating so many things, her mind seemed to stay on her grandparents. Shannon was sorry for not spending more time with them. As she reviewed that last ten years, she recognized that once she started to get involved in school activities and friends, everything seemed to become more important than family.

She got up and went into the kitchen to make some coffee. Shannon spoke aloud to her empty apartment, "Now I long for a few more hours with my grandfather. I long for him to hug me once more and take me out on the lake in his boat. Seems like people leave, one way or another, and those left behind must find a way to get by."

Shannon took her coffee, went back to her new sofa, and admired all the furniture her father purchased for her as a graduation present. He had to go out of town on business and couldn't go to her graduation ceremony, but she was not surprised. That's what he did: Pay up but not show up. That was something she would never understand. She knew if she thought too long about her father, too many memories would come flooding back, along with emotions that she would rather not revisit.

Shannon knew what she must do. She needed to go see Grandma. It was getting later in the day, but she could wait no longer. She sent her grandmother a text to make sure she would be home and waited for her reply. After she received an answer, she packed a bag and set out to make the two-hour drive.

She didn't arrive until nine in the evening. Her grandmother was waiting and greeted her with those hugs that Shannon missed. Grandma Lou was thrilled to have Shannon come and stay. Lou loved her grandchildren very much, and even though they were all grown and didn't come around very often, she kept busy with the many things she loved to do. She was always busy with art projects, reading, and activities with friends and church. Lou was very thankful for every text or phone call she received from her grandbabies, as she lovingly still called them. But Lou knew they now had lives of their own, and their visits would be few, "That's life," she would say.

Shannon remembered when they were little, their grandparents' house was the destination. It's where they all wanted to go. Her grandparents would plan every minute of their stays to make sure their grandbabies had fun. Shannon fondly remembered that her grandma would always pray with them when they went to bed. It made Shannon feel loved. *Now here I am once again,* she thought. *It feels like I am supposed to be here. I feel at peace.*

Grandma helped Shannon put her things in the guest room and took her into the kitchen for a late-night snack and some light conversation. Shannon had many things she wanted to ask her grandmother, but not tonight. They had all weekend to catch up.

Tonight she just wanted to feel her love and to sleep once more in that soft bed she had always enjoyed. Tonight all Shannon needed was a retreat from her cluttered mind and a rest for her weary body. She felt like she had been on a treadmill at full speed for the last four years, and she desperately needed to slow down. As she drifted off to sleep, Shannon knew that she had come to the right place.

Morning came shining through the open window. Shannon could hear the birds singing and cars driving by. She had slept well. As she stretched, she could hear the familiar sound of Grandma's radio playing in the kitchen as she cooked up one of Shannon's favorite breakfasts, pancakes with real maple syrup. Shannon quickly jumped in the shower and then dressed and hurried downstairs. There, Grandma stood in her jeans and T-shirt, moving to the sound of some upbeat Christian song Shannon had never heard before. "Grandma, I didn't think you still had it in you!"

"Well, I'm not that old," Lou said with a giggle. "You have been away awhile, but not that long. I'm still loving my tunes! Remember when I used to get you up dancing around the room with me?"

"Yes, I remember," Shannon said. She laughed.

They ate breakfast together and caught up on each other's lives. Shannon told her grandma about her new job. "Remember, Grandma, it was that place where I interned when I was in college. I liked it there, and they recently offered me a job. I start in two weeks. I wish it was closer to you, but it's only two hours away. I was glad to get something that close to you and Mom!"

"I know you will do very well, Shannon. You know you can come stay with me any weekend you want."

"I know," Shannon said. "I will more often. I promise."

When they finished breakfast, Shannon helped her grandmother clean up the kitchen, and then they went out to walk through Lou's flower gardens. Lou, sensing something was wrong, asked Shannon, "How are you really feeling?"

Shannon let out a sign and began. "Oh, Grandma, I'm so unhappy, and I feel so empty. That's one reason I came to visit. I needed you to help me figure out some things. I can't go to Mom. She barely keeps it together herself."

Lou turned and waved her hand in the direction of the porch swing and suggested they go sit for a while. "Shannon, I know your mom is still hurting from your father leaving. I pray for her all the time. We talk some, but she's built a wall and won't let anyone in. It's like she holds onto the hurt as if it is a safety blanket, and I can't get her to let go of it. I pray for her every day. God will make a way. I know He will!"

Lou went on, "Shannon, I wonder if you are still holding on to that pain as well. Unforgiveness and emotional pain are like heavy weights on your heart. They block joy and happiness from being able to take hold and grow. It is like this landscape mulch on my flower bed. It blocks the sun from the weeds and the seeds from the soil, so they can't grow."

"I know, Grandma. Every time my mind goes back to those feelings, I just quit thinking about it. I thought I had it under control, but maybe I don't."

"Shannon, you have to get rid of the bitterness that has developed from the pain so that you are free to find happiness. I do believe it may be some of what is holding you back."

"How do I do that, Grandma?"

"Oh, sweetie, you pray to the Lord to heal you and help you forgive. Remember, I taught you how to pray."

Shannon sighed, knowing she had not prayed in a long time. "OK, Grandma. I will try, but I really came to find out what makes you happy. Grandma, even when Grandpa died you were sad, yet you still seemed content with life."

"Yes, Shannon. "I am happy. I am happy because the Lord fills me with His joy. Romans 15:13 says, "May the God of hope fill you with all joy and peace as you trust in Him, so that you may overflow with hope by the power of the Holy Spirit.

"Shannon, the Lord imparts joy in us through His Son, Jesus, and His Holy Spirit. He also opens our eyes so we are able to recognize all the things in our lives that bring us happiness. Sweetheart, the way it works for me is when I see or feel or even taste something good, I am grateful, and I praise the Lord with a sincere heart. Then my mind and emotions pick up a joyful presence and a realization of how much I enjoy those things, and I feel happy. Does that make sense?"

Shannon thought for a few minutes before answering. "I guess. But what are the things that make you happy? I can't seem to recognize any for myself."

"My dear Shannon, you are at a low point, aren't you? OK, well you know I do a lot of thinking, therefore I try to recognize every little good thing in each day. But my basic list of things that make me happy would include my relationship with the Lord, family and friends, my hobbies, my music, nature and all its beauty, animals, and the like. Other things, like my home, food, clothes, and things that make me comfortable. You know from staying with me that I like my comfortable things, like all those soft throws and blankets, comfy beds, my fireplace, and, of course, a hot cup of tea. Shannon, there are just so many good things. I know this sounds silly, but somehow in my head I combine all those good things together with my many wonderful memories, and I feel very happy, blessed, and satisfied. Even when I think about your grandfather or my parents who are gone, I am able to smile and relive special times I shared with them. Those memories also bring me joy and warm my heart. All these things are gifts from God, Shannon. They are for our enjoyment. And with a thankful heart, we give Him praise."

"Grandma, why is it that I could not see all this for myself? Why did I have to come here and have you explain it to me?"

Lou put her arm around her granddaughter and pulled her close. "Shannon, unless you walk with the Lord, you walk blindly. You walk in a dark world, where there is fun but not happiness. Where things made by man are advertised to bring happiness, but in reality, they are meaningless, leaving you feeling empty after a time. From what you have told me so far, it sounds like you already know what that's all about.

"Shannon, we need to spend some time in prayer today. You need to ask the Lord Jesus to come in and take control of your life and your emotions. Then we need to ask the Lord to help you forgive your father and ask Him to come in, heal that pain, and release you from it. I think it might also be a good idea to make a list of the good things in your life so that you can visually see them on paper and begin, one by one, to praise the Lord for them. I know you will leave here this weekend feeling much better."

"Grandma, I need a change. I think I am ready to let go of everything inside that's ugly and harmful to me. I thought I could bury it, but now I see it's toxic, and I want to get rid of it. I want to start my new job and my future without this baggage. I want so much to be happy and content, just like you, Grandma. You have always been a good example for us all."

"Shannon, do you know how I came to be this way?"

"No, I have no idea. You never said."

Lou got up from the swing, walked toward her flowers, and looked over all that she had been blessed with. "I was taught about the Lord at home as a child. But when I grew up, I had to go out and do it all wrong first because of my stubborn, sinful nature. I had a grandmother and a wonderful set of parents who prayed hard for me. Once I learned failure and rejection in the most painful way, I finally came to embrace what I ran away from, God and family. See, Shannon, sometimes we have to make a mess of things before we find out there is only one road to happiness, and it is through the Creator of all things good. Once I committed my life to the Lord, many things changed for the better. For me, it changed quickly. It may not be that way for everyone, but I think it is for most. My physical and spiritual eyes see clearly now, and I can easily recognize how blessed I am. And that makes me very happy! You see, I'm not blind anymore, and my heart is open. That has made all the difference in my life."

Shannon and her grandmother spent the rest of the weekend praying and talking about many things. She left Monday morning with a different outlook on her life and her future. She left behind anger and bitterness and embraced the joy of the Lord.

As she got into her car and headed out, Shannon knew that even though she had asked the Lord to help her forgive her father, she needed to have a difficult conversation with her dad. On the long drive home, Shannon had time to think, and at one point proclaimed aloud, "My dad either needs to show up when we plan things, or we must come to some other arrangement." She could not stand his broken promises any longer. The disappointment was just too much to bear. She loved him, but she needed to guard her heart so she could have a joy-filled life. His monetary gifts would not and could not make up for the real father-daughter relationship she longed for. As much as she dreaded the conversation, which would be by phone of course, Shannon needed to have it so the pain would not continue. "Sometimes," she said to herself, "I just have to take care of things and not hide them under the proverbial rug! My happiness depends on it."

> Nehemiah said, "Go and enjoy choice food and sweet drinks, and send some to those who have nothing prepared. This day is holy to our Lord. Do not grieve, for the joy of the Lord is your strength." (Nehemiah 8:10)

> Happiness is fleeting, but joy is eternal. Happiness has to do with our happenings, which change all the time. But joy from the Lord is unchanging. (Pastor Steve Harman)

A Perfect Day

What is a perfect day? A perfect day is when several things that are meaningful and enjoyable come together in an extraordinary way to make it very significant. A perfect day for one person may not be the same for another. But for me, most of my perfect days seem to have all the following elements: a sunny day, spending time with someone very special to me, doing something out of the ordinary, and feeling well. It is a day that I look back on with happiness and say, "That was a perfect day!"

I have had many wonderful days with family and friends, but perfect days are a little extra special; they burn a memory in my brain. Let me tell you about one very special day that I will cherish for the rest of my life.

Just a few days before my mother was to turn ninety, I took her clothes shopping because our family was hosting an open house birthday party for her, and she wanted something new to wear. There were a few things that made that day extra special. Mom had just recovered from cataract surgery and was able to see everything clearly for the first time in a long time. She had also been having mini strokes and was beginning to get really confused and sometimes hard to deal with. It was difficult at times for her to get past her confusion and to be in the moment. To put it mildly, it was becoming a very sad and exhausting situation, as many people with elderly parents can understand. But on this warm, sunny day in October, she was able to see all the leaves and fall flowers, and she was in her right mind all day long. It was an amazing, joy-filled day for me because I had been grieving the loss of her ability to comprehend and converse with me. That day was truly a gift from God. Little did I know, a week later everything would change forever.

Mother and I drove to town through the country, and she commented on every beautiful thing she saw. She was laughing and so happy. It was truly amazing to watch her as she sat in the front seat beside me, so animated and youthful. We talked and laughed just like we had years before; it was wonderful. Shopping was fun, and I helped her find the perfect outfit for the party. She had so much fun trying on clothes and enjoying everything she was able to see with those new eyes. A few days later, we had her party, and she was still in good shape, happy and talking with relatives and friends and looking beautiful in her new clothes. This is a memory that blesses me to this day. I still have those clothes of hers; I can't seem to part with them. They are earthly reminders of a heavenly time when God gave me a very precious gift, one last wonderful, normal, mother-daughter outing with my mother.

About one week later, Mom began breaking bones, and we found out she had osteoporosis. She was in terrible pain all the time. Between the pain, the drugs, and all the other stuff she had to go through, I don't remember her having many lucid moments after that. She broke more bones before she died that next year.

I praise God for that one very precious day. It's funny, we never know how God will put situations together to bless us. In order to seize these opportunities, we have to be ready and willing to put aside time, be in the moment, and soak up the joy. Because of our busy lives, I believe we sometimes miss some perfect days. I know deep down inside that they are little gifts from God that show us how much He cares.

There is another perfect day in history that God put in place. An event that would change lives forever, Easter. The sun came up, the tomb of our Lord was empty, and humankind was given the most precious of all gifts, the opportunity to receive eternal life through Jesus Christ's suffering, death, and resurrection.

After the Sabbath, at dawn on the first day of the week, Mary Magdalene and the other Mary went to look at the tomb. (Matthew 28:1)

The angel said to the women, "Do not be afraid, for I know that you are looking for Jesus, who was crucified. He is not here; He has risen, just as He said. Come and see the place where He lay. Then go quickly and tell His disciples; He has risen from the dead and is going ahead of you into Galilee. There you will see Him. Now I have told you." (Matthew 28:5–7)

These Bible verses explain this remarkable event.

For God was pleased to have all His fullness dwell in Him, and through Him to reconcile to Himself all things, whether things on earth or things in heaven, by making peace through his blood, shed on the cross. Once you were alienated from God and were enemies in your minds because of your evil behavior. But now He Has reconciled you by Christ's physical body through death to present you holy in His sight, without blemish and free from accusation if you continue in your faith, established and firm, and do not move from the hope held out in the gospel. This is the gospel that you heard and that has been proclaimed to every creature under heaven, and of which I, Paul, have become a servant. (Colossians 1:19–23)

Perfection, to me, means all good things coming together in a way that I am not able to find dissatisfaction in any object, event, or person. I know that I can only perceive perfection because of Christ living in me.

Without Him, I can be critical and hard to please, therefore giving up my ability to find joy and satisfaction. This would make it very hard to have any perfect days. In many cases, for us to be able to see perfection, I believe we must first be perfected by the shed blood of Jesus Christ. We need that positive attitude and perfect love that He provides.

My hope is that God's perfect love finds its way into your heart and that your eyes will be open to His wonderful opportunities so that you can see perfection when it comes your way.

The Secrets to Enduring Love

A great marriage is a treasured gift that a husband and wife give to each other.

My husband and I were each married once before. In both our first marriages, we found ourselves in situations that were out of our control. Divorce is an ugly and difficult event, but God has a way of taking broken things and making something beautiful from them. Such is the case with my present marriage of thirty-four years to my wonderful husband. I love the following verse:

> The Lord is close to the brokenhearted and saves those
> who are crushed in spirit. (Psalm 34:18)

I wrote the following poem for our wedding.

Kaleidoscope of Our Lives

Shades of color broken by the light, broken images of our lives.
Shattered dreams broken like glass, painful memories all in the past.
Change in direction, timing, and light, the pieces begin to fit together
as does our lives.

Only from pain is beauty born; a twist in
time, and new people are formed.
As a kaleidoscope, the shades and pieces begin to fit together
to create something very beautiful that has finally come together.

I believe there are bad marriages, good marriages, and great ones. I can say from experience that marriage can be the worst or the best thing that could ever happen to a person, so choose a mate carefully, and involve the Lord in your decisions. I have done it both ways. It's not too hard to guess which marriage was the one where I ignored what God thought and which one I prayed about. As my parents would have said, "Many of us have to graduate from the school of hard knocks."

After we had been married many years, our youngest son asked us what our secret was to a good marriage. These are some of what I have experienced and observed about marriage over the last forty-five years.

One key to our success is that neither of us is selfish or self-centered. A relationship does not work well if one or both people are self-centered. My husband and I put the other person's needs above our own.

We care so much that we make it a priority to make each other's life the best that it can be! We share a level of happiness that most people do not achieve because they are not willing to love anyone more than they love themselves.

Another thing I know to be true is that when a person is rude, he or she usually receives a rude reaction. For every action, there is a reaction; and in marriage, reactions come quickly! So if we are kind most of the time, we will get kindness in return. Of course, the exception is if you are married to a totally self-absorbed person. Then you have to do what you can and give that person to God every day in prayer.

I find that it is fun to make people happy. I love to do things for my spouse, children, and friends that will bring them joy and make their lives easier. I do things without expecting something in return. That is the key. If we do things expecting something in return, we are setting ourselves up for disappointment and hurt. We have to know in our hearts that we did what was pleasing in God's sight, and let Him work through that situation.

We should never base our happiness on just people. They are human, and they are fallible. We must first derive our happiness from God. What

I mean is, we enjoy the gift of love given to us from other people, but we are not to depend on it totally. We have to be happy with ourselves and our lives through God's lens of love.

By putting God at the forefront of our lives, He gives us the ability to put the needs of others ahead of our own. Being in God's Word, the Bible, makes it easier for us to be kind and patient and to ask for and give forgiveness. Look at it this way. God is a positive force in our lives, and the world is mostly negative. We will become what we spend most of our time involved in. The world says, "You are worth it. You are number one, so do it your way, have your fun, do your thing. You deserve it!" All these clichés send subliminal messages to our brains to disregard everyone else. So in the name of having it all, eyes wander, hearts are untrue, and deception and selfishness take center stage, while the innocent are shattered like broken glass.

To have a really good marriage, we must work at it. To be good at our jobs or our hobbies, we have to put a lot of effort into them, so why would we expect our marriages to be any different? A good marriage just doesn't drop out of the sky. A couple needs to make it their vocation. It must be their main occupation, and they must regard it as worthy of great dedication.

Here are a few tips from my life for creating something beautiful and lasting:

1. Put God in your marriage. A great marriage consists of God, your spouse, and you. Make God and your spouse a priority. Though one may be overpowered, two can defend themselves. A cord of three strands is not quickly broken (Ecclesiastes 4:12).

2. Plan time away together, even if it just for a day. The planning is part of the fun, and it gives a couple something to look forward to. Spending time alone together is very important. Some people call them dates. We have had so many wonderful mini-vacations, camping trips, bike rides, and so on. A couple needs time to have fun and laugh together to keep that spark alive.

3. Involve family and friends in your marriage. There is much joy in sharing your life with others. It seems to bring some stability,

and it gives everyone the opportunity to make great memories. Memories create layers of joy.

4. Take care of each other in sickness and in health. Also, hold each other's hands. Tell them you love them often, if not every day. That constant touch and affirmation goes a long way to keep love alive and make your spouse feel loved and cherished.

5. Become a good listener. If you love this person, what he or she has to say should be important. Learn to compromise; learn to let go. Being right all the time is not as important as being in a relationship for a lifetime. If a conversation gets to a point where you can't get anywhere, take time to cool off. Another couple I know suggest using a time-out signal that the two of you have agreed on beforehand. You may also consider writing a letter to your partner. He or she can read your point of view without your presence, when there is no conversation. In that way, your spouse can take the time to think things over.

6. Be sure to pray. This is so very important. Pray for your spouse's safety, health, your relationship, everything. Take it all to God every day. By doing this, you are putting a protective hedge around your spouse and your marriage.

7. Relax, lighten up, be able to go with the flow. Once in a while, something comes up, plans have to change, and it's not worth getting upset about. It always seems to work out fine. Most of the time my husband and I know each other's plans because we are pretty good at communicating. Communication is the key to success. We are also really good at encouraging each other's hobbies and time with friends. It is very comfortable living in a loving and accepting environment.

8. Respect each other. This is huge and lacking in many marriages. I can't believe the way I hear people talk to each other! Don't say things to your spouse that would hurt him or her. Just don't do it! Why do it? This is being ugly and mean. It's not funny, and those things stick whether you think they do or not. If we love our spouses, we will respect their feelings, abilities, and opinions.

9. We may not always agree, but we don't need to destroy our spouses in the process. This destroys the marriage. In everything, we must

treat others the way we would want to be treated. This is not a sitcom or a game show; it is your real life.

We are uniquely made; we were not meant to be the same. I have noticed that as the years go by, we do seem to grow more in step with each other. Here are some great words of wisdom on this subject:

> Don't try to change your spouse. The only person you can change is yourself and only with God's help. We may want to consider that we are different because God wants us to complete one another, not compete with one another. (Pastor Steve Harman)

These two Bible verses come to mind as I am writing about love. They are the secret to a great marriage or any relationship you want to be successful.

So in everything do to others what you would have them do to you, for this sums up the law and the Prophets. (Matthew 7:12)

> Love is patient and kind. Love is not jealous or boastful or proud or rude. It does not demand its own way. It is not irritable, and it keeps no record of being wronged. It does not rejoice about injustice but rejoices whenever the truth wins out. Love never gives up, never loses faith, is always hopeful, and endures through every circumstance. (1 Corinthians 13:4–7 NLT)

In conclusion, as the old saying goes, if you want a good friend, be a good friend. I say if you want a good spouse, you have to be a good spouse. Please know if your marriage is not perfect, God is the heart and life-changer. Give it all to Him in prayer, and do your part. Enduring love is possible and easily achievable when it is blessed by God.

Blended Family of Books

I have long thought of my life as a book. Each chapter is a different year, a different set of adventures, with challenges that I have enjoyed and overcome. My life had a beginning, just like a book, and some day it will have an end. What happens in the middle is just like a good novel. It's all a mystery not to be totally understood until the finale.

Most of the time, we don't have a clue what might happen next, but we live and trust that it will all work out. When we get married and start a family, we begin to add books (children) and start a series. Sometimes the original series stops as life gets interrupted.

When a family unit changes because of death or divorce, so does the original life series. When a parent remarries, the lives of two families now combine into one to become what I call a "blended family of books." This is very difficult to do because the stories have already been started. There were many things established with different people in those two families. And now everything has changed. It all started one way and then, like a train, was diverted onto a new track, in a new direction, and into a new territory yet to be discovered.

I became a mother at twenty-five. A few years later I divorced, remarried, and became a stepmother at thirty. In theory, blending two families together sounds like a wonderfully easy thing to do, but it is not! Taking care of stepchildren's physical needs is not so different. But gaining love and respect from those children is because that love and respect is already with the ones who gave them life. For a while, I was the babysitter and Dad's wife. It took a lot of hard work and prayer to get the love I longed for from my stepchildren. As parents, our own children suffer a bit because at one time, they had our full attention, and now they have to share us with these new people in their lives.

When my husband and I got married, I looked at the situation as if I were one of his children and asked myself how I would want to be treated. I knew to do this because my mother taught me to look at each situation from all angles and to put myself in the other person's place.

Children can tell if we are insincere. They can sense if we are really trying to love them or wishing they were not there at all. Children will act up because they are thrown into a situation where they have no control and, most likely, no choice. They are probably in turmoil and pain, not understanding what has happened or why. Children may fear that this new person in their lives may hurt them or that they will have to go through another breakup if this new situation does not work out.

I hate to write about this, but sometimes the other parent, the one not in this new family unit, may say or do things to drive a wedge between the stepparent and the children. You can't change another person. From what I have lived and observed, only time, prayer, and your sincere commitment to those children will change the situation. This will challenge you and show you just what you are made of, and you will need to stay in constant prayer to get through it.

I would have to say that divorce is a vehicle of fear, pain, and anger that takes all involved on a long and difficult ride into the great unknown. Now that I am well past all that, I would like to offer a little wisdom to help make the next person's ride a little less bumpy.

My suggestions:

1. Cover each day and each person with prayer. You are going to need God's help.
2. Work really hard at treating your stepchildren like your own. Never treat your own better. I don't believe that to be godly at all, and that is not the way any person would want to be treated. What you do for your own, also do for your stepchildren. "Whoever

welcomes one of these little children *in my name welcomes me; and whoever welcomes me does not welcome me but the one who sent me*" (Mark 9:37).

3.   Do fun things that include all the children. When we got married, our children were four, five, and six, and I started playing bake shop with them. I would conduct fun, silly interviews and hire them as baker, dough maker, cookie cutter, and so on, and we would bake together. I even put pictures of them up on the wall with their job titles just for fun and as a visual reminder of those good times together. They really enjoyed those type of activities. It's basically like a sport; after a while, they go from being individual players to a team.

4.   Commit to this new marriage. These children need to know you are in it for the long haul so they can begin to feel a sense of security. When they can see that you are committed, it will help lessen the initial spiteful behavior directed toward the stepparent. After they figure out that you are there to stay, things will begin to calm down, provided you are showing love and kindness to them.

5.   Come into total agreement with your spouse on how to discipline the children. Some aspects of discipline work better being enforced by the biological parent. Always discipline everyone fairly, or there will be resentment, and you will have problems. No one says discipline has to be harsh, but it is necessary in order to raise law-abiding, loving, and kind people who know how to obey both of you and obey the Lord. Yes, we may feel for what they are going through, but it's not wise to baby the children and let them be disobedient or disrespectful. They will have many difficult times throughout their lives, and they must be taught how to handle themselves without throwing tantrums, breaking the law, and hurting others or themselves. Dealing with these challenges is a great time to teach children how to get through things by relying on God. The most important component of all is that they are grounded in God's love and the love of family:

Children, obey your parents in everything, for this pleases
the Lord. Fathers, do not embitter your children, or they
will become discouraged. (Colossians 3:20, 21)

6. Be realistic. Your feelings are going to get hurt a little more as
    a stepparent than as a biological parent. Remember, they are
    children, not adults, and they don't think like adults. They need
    to have boundaries, of course, but they often do and say things
    that they don't even know could hurt you. In many cases, the Lord
    is the only place you should run to, so commit your life to prayer
    and studying the Bible. Unloading or venting to other people will
    often make them treat who you are complaining about differently,
    even poorly, so be careful. It is better to take refuge in the Lord
    than to trust in humans (Psalm 118:8).

7. Try to find a few hours or a day every now and again to be
    with one child at a time. They will feel important and loved, not
    forgotten in the new crowd.

8. Find a hobby or something you love to do where you can find
    some quality time for yourself. For me, it was gardening. I could be
    right outside the door, or they could be outside with me, but they
    let me be. Maybe they thought I would make them pull weeds or
    something. Anyway, it worked, and I loved it. I received joy from
    my gardening and a little me time when I really needed it. You can
    even ask God to show you what that could be for you.

9. Don't say bad things about their parents. That will go a long way
    to help the relationship. It's not easy, and I know I was not perfect,
    but it was well worth the effort.

10. Do your best to get along with the divorced parents. If there are
    problems, it's best for your spouse to work it out with the ex than
    for you to tackle the situation. Once in a while, you may have to
    team up to talk to them.

11. *Key:* If you really love your new spouse, you will love their children
    too. Children do not go away. They are jewels for a whole life to
    be treasured while you are raising them and in the future, when
    they come home with their own babies. When you sign on to blend
    your lives together, you sign on for the whole package, whether

you've thought about it or not. You want your new spouse to love your children, and he or she want you to love theirs; it can truly be a blessing if you allow it to be.

12. If you are able to work hard and love your spouse's children like your own, you will win over the heart and soul of your mate like nothing else you could ever do because your spouse's children mean the world to him or her.

13. Children grow up very quickly and take on busy lives of their own. As a couple, you and your spouse will have many years together to enjoy, so work to protect your marriage for the future and the very reason you fell in love in the first place. Carve out time for you as a couple, like date nights and time alone. It is very important.

14. When the children grow up and have children of their own, you are no longer "step" this or that. You are just Grandma and Grandpa to those wonderful babies. It is your reward and truly life's greatest blessing.

I have to say blending our families together was one of the hardest and most rewarding things I have ever experienced. I shed many tears, prayed an enormous number of prayers, and worked extremely hard to try to be fair to all our children. I can honestly say with all my heart that it was worth every minute, every tear, and every struggle. I remember many of those days seemed to last forty-eight hours instead of twenty-four, and I had to tell myself, "This too shall pass." And it did. Now they are all grown, and I miss many things about those years. As a new family unit, we shared many fun camping trips and vacations. My husband and I were Scout leaders and coaches for them, and we attended their many activities and events. We intentionally made memories, worked at enjoying and valuing each other, and at making our own unique story.

Would it have been God's plan for two families to split up to make another? No, I don't think so. But you know what? God is excellent at putting broken things together to create something beautiful from the pieces left behind. Looking back, we were successful because both of us loved the Lord, loved each other, and valued and loved our children. So I guess you could say the theme through all our books is love, with God as our example and guide. If there ever was a verse that described how to be a spouse, parent, or stepparent it is in 1 Corinthians 13:4–7.

We live in a world full of sin and sorrow, and not everything we attempt to do turns out right. Sometimes things are just out of our control. No one knows another person's life or another person's pain, but everybody needs love and forgiveness, not judgment. If we are given the chance to positively affect another person's life, consider it a divine opportunity.

God is the key to success because when we live in the grace of God, believing and trusting, all things *are* possible, as in my favorite Bible verse, Philippians 4:13.

Children:
A Treasure Entrusted to Us

I love children. They are so full of energy and laughter, and their smiles just melt my heart. There isn't anything sweeter than the sound of a child's laughter. To be a mother and have the privilege of enjoying those little arms and hands around my neck was a great source of joy for me. I believe being a mother was truly my highest calling and my greatest reward. I remember being in the hospital and the doctor handing me our baby for the first time; it took my breath away. It was what I would call a heavenly moment, a true gift from God.

> Don't you see that children are God's best gift? The fruit of the womb His generous legacy. Like a warrior's fistful of arrows are children of a vigorous youth. Oh, how blessed are you parents, with your quivers full of children! (Psalm 127:3–5 MSG)

My childhood was pretty good. Even though my parents were in their forties when I was born, I felt very loved and cherished. I had six brothers several years older than I, so when they were grown, I had my parents to myself. I have several nieces and nephews close to me in age. It has always been a blessing to be part of a large family. In school, there were activities I missed out on because my parents were older, but in hindsight, those things were really not important. It did not make or break my life in any way not to have done them. What was important to my parents had heavenly significance, not worldly importance. They were extremely concerned with where we children were going when we died and how we treated other people and ourselves. Sports and other activities, or having the latest things, were not a high priority to my mother and father. As a child, I accepted but did not fully understand that, but I do now.

I believe that as parents, we are entrusted with the responsibility of molding our children into productive, nurturing, and caring individuals who have the assurance that they are someone very special in God's eyes. They must know God has a purpose and a plan for each person. They need to know that they were not a mistake, no matter the circumstances of their arrival. Planned or unplanned, all children are known and loved by God.

> For You created my inmost being; You knit me together in my mother's womb. I praise You because I am fearfully and wonderfully made; Your works are wonderful, I know that full well. My frame was not hidden from You when I was made in the secret place, when I was woven together in the depths of the earth. Your eyes saw my unformed body; all the days ordained for me were written in Your book before one of them came to be. (Psalm 139:13–16)

I firmly believe that as parents it is very important to be the wall, a safe boundary around our children. It is a wall that keeps them walking down a safe path to a good life. This wall keeps them from plummeting into the deep, dangerous canyon that lies on either side. Sadly, we all know of children who have fallen from drugs, suicide, and so on and lost their lives. We also know some who have fallen yet are clinging onto the side of the cliff and can still be rescued. For many, their futures will be difficult. For some reason, when I was a young parent, I always called myself "the wall." It was the wall that guided my children with wisdom, experience, and love as they journeyed and grew along life's path. My wall provided shelter for them from the storms of life.

Yes, I remember them beating against the wall with all their might, wanting to go to parties or other activities their peers were involved in. Sometimes an overwhelming sense would come over me, and I would know in my heart that their plans were not good or safe. Years later, I would discover that I had often been correct not to let them participate in certain activities. That was more than my gut talking to me; it was the Holy Spirit protecting my babies. Oh, there were arguments and so forth, but I kept telling myself, "Be strong. Be the wall!" I know I received the strength to be the wall through my time in prayer and Bible reading. That was the only way I felt I could persevere and not let down the wall.

Please know I'm not in any way saying the wall involves being abusive. It is engaging and caring, observant, guiding and respectful, but firm in its commitment to keep children safe physically, emotionally, and spiritually. There are many ways to discipline children, and they do not have to be harsh or abusive. But discipline is necessary for any child's well-being and future. Discipline helps to create a well-behaved, self-controlled person who reaps blessings throughout life.

> To discipline a child produces wisdom, but a mother is disgraced by an undisciplined child. (Proverbs 29:15 NLT)

> Discipline your children and they will give you peace of mind and will make your heart glad. (Proverbs 29:17 NLT)

Here's the raw and honest truth. Are you ready for it? We cannot be the wall for our children if we don't love them more than we love ourselves. We have to own that purest form of love that says, "I will give my life to protect you," and mean it. This is what allows parents to properly build and maintain the wall. Plain and simple, it takes hard work to be the kind of parent our children need and the kind of parent God asks us to be. He entrusted us with a precious treasure of great value and eternal significance. My children were worth every single ounce of energy I had to give. Was I always liked by my children? Of course not! No child likes to hear, "No," but it's a lifesaving word in many cases.

I learned that being a parent is not all about being a friend, as some television shows may portray. Those producers can write any outcome in a script and make it look good. No, being a parent is about being your child's guardian and mentor. It is about establishing a close bonding relationship, the relationship that comes about with a loving and an intentional effort to seek daily communication. This develops from time spent with each other. It's about what we do with and for them on a regular basis. The true friend relationship with our children will come when they are adults. But while they are young, being a dedicated parent is more important than being a friend.

As parents, we are responsible for helping our children establish firm foundations for their futures. This foundation must be based on values that we establish in our families. These values come from the Word of God spoken from our lips and lived out in the examples we display in front of our children. They are also formed by the people, places, and things we allowed them to be involved with as they grew. Think about it. Would we allow our children to step out in front of a car? Of course not! We often fear for a child's physical safety, so why would we not fear for their spiritual safety on the earth and their eternal futures? I, for one, want to see my children in heaven. And I want them to have a good life on earth by staying out of trouble and treating people with love and respect as God intended. As people who took parenting very seriously, these were the most important things my husband and I could instill in our children.

Some of you may wonder if our grown children's lives are perfect. I have to say no. No one's life is perfect; this is earth, not heaven. What I can say with confidence is that they know and understand boundaries and consequences. They know what love feels like, and they are able to give what they have been given. Our children know where to go to find the source of all hope, peace, guidance, and love: God Almighty, through His Son, Jesus Christ.

I believe that God is the lighthouse, and my husband and I are just the caretakers. Even though our grown children may get tossed about in a few storms, they have been taught how to follow the light of the lighthouse. It's always there, always shining, always waiting to guide them safely back to the shore. No matter what age we are, we are all children to God and in need of the light and love He provides. It can relieve our panic and calm the stormy seas until we get to go home to be with Him.

Oh, how I wish a lot of people loved children as much as God does. But the deceiver, Satan, has blinded and hardened hearts to believe that a beautiful little child is an inconvenience, annoyance, or something to use or discard. Can you imagine instead a world where all children were loved and treasured? Think about how that would affect the generations to come. By being a good parent, we are paying it forward, and we are loving God by caring for those souls He entrusted to our care. In today's world, I have observed:

- Many adults have quit believing in God or never learned of His love. Therefore, they never establish any kind of foundation that would keep them from doing the unthinkable.
- People in today's society often worship themselves and their pleasures. There just isn't much room for the needs of others.
- Because of the first two, the next generation is never shown love and respect and are unable to give what they have never received.

The only thing that can rectify this disorder is for people who know love to begin to show it to those who do not. Again, it's hard work, but look at our world. There are so many suffering in silence. If we were among them, wouldn't we long to find a lighthouse and a few good caretakers?

Once Again

Once Again

In the quiet of the day I feel you near.

My eyes behold a majestic sky, carefully painted

with your gentle hand. I feel strange, everything

is so temporary, so fleeting. Your message gently

filters in my ear as the music softly plays.

I am drawn to think of you for a while.

I am drawn to look closely at all that is around me.

I need not see the wonder to validate your existence,

but to focus. Out of a tired existence, I praise your name.

Out of a noisey day, I lay down my burdens.

Out of this sinful shell, I once again retire my

cluttered mind. Once again you refresh and forgive.

Once again, I will rest for a time, then continue to live.

Living in a Spirit-Filled World

Have you ever experienced a feeling of joy and wonder as you look out at the ocean, beautiful mountains, or gardens full of brilliant colors? What about those precious, tear-jerking moments of joy like holding your newborn baby for the first time? Now, on the opposite end of the spectrum, have you ever been in a place that didn't feel right, like it was not safe? Have you ever been around a person who made you very uncomfortable? If so, then you have had spiritual encounters. You have either been filled with joy and love from the Father of creation, or you have felt the dark constricting spirit of evil that puts fear in us and makes us want to get away. Our world is a spiritual world. It is a world we can often feel and see through the behaviors of others.

> For our struggle is not against flesh and blood, but against the rulers, against the authorities, against the powers of this dark world and against the spiritual forces of evil in the heavenly realms. (Ephesians 6:12)

Let me tell you about an experience I had when I was thirteen. This brush with evil seared a memory in my brain. That year around Halloween, our church's volunteer youth leaders decided that we would have a Halloween party, and they proceeded to build a haunted house in the church basement. I did not help with the setup but went innocently enough to the party to have some fun. As I was walking into the church, I began to encounter something that made me feel very ill at ease, but I shook it off. As I entered the room where the party was, I felt like something was enveloping me, tightening around me. I was also feeling a keen sense of anxiousness, as if two opposing beings were boxing it out inside my chest. Now at thirteen, I knew about God, but I didn't know anything about spiritual warfare until that moment. No one had to explain it to me; I knew. It was more tangible and more real than actually seeing a physical battle play out in front of my eyes. It was all-consuming, and I made some excuse and left the party. I had to get as far away from there as possible! I walked several blocks before the feeling let up. I don't remember if I told my mom about it, but I know I prayed. I had a very different opinion of Halloween after that.

Fast-forward about seventeen years. I was married with three children who wanted to participate in trick or treat like all the other children. But I remembered my encounter at thirteen and was not thrilled about letting them take part in this tradition.

My husband was not keen on all that candy, so we agreed to just take the children out to eat and satisfy them with a little candy. We did not allow them to take part in the door-to-door ritual. Over the years, it was difficult to keep them from participating. When I was just about to cave, some of that anxiety I felt at thirteen would return until I said no.

For whatever reason, God gave me a discerning spirit and showed me that Halloween is really not harmless. It is a holiday for evil spirits to roam free and create havoc in people's lives. As a parent, we sometimes just cave and let our kids do things that seems to be harmless. If it isn't going to make a difference five years from now, why fight about it, right? Well, this was one area that the Holy Spirit would not let me slide on because it very well could make a huge difference in my children's spiritual well-being and eternal futures. I was not about to portray Halloween as a good, safe, fun thing for my children when I knew better. There is much debate about this in the church, and frankly, people don't want to hear it. Many times it's because people do not study the Bible and are ignorant of spiritual things. They see this holiday as harmless because, "Everybody is doing it."

Nevertheless, the Bible clearly speaks of God's Spirit, the Holy Spirit, and of demonic spirits of Satan in this world.

> But the Advocate, the Holy Spirit, whom the Father will send in my name, will teach you all things and will remind you of everything I have said to you. (John 14:26)

> Be alert and of sober mind. Your enemy the devil prowls around like a roaring lion *looking for someone to devour.* (1 Peter 5:8)

> They are demonic spirits that perform signs, and they go out to the kings of the whole world, to gather them for the battle on the great day of God Almighty. (Revelation 16:14)

> Have nothing to do with the fruitless deeds of darkness, but rather expose them. (Ephesians 5:11)

There are many evil spirits that can come and torment a person without that person realizing what is happening. A person can have a spirit of infirmity (sickness and disease), jealousy, rage, unforgiveness, defeat, fear, anxiety, hate, and so on. How does a person get such spirits? I believe we open the door to them. They have to be given permission to come in. Just like setting up a haunted house in a church, where they were invited in, unknowingly, by our young youth group leaders. Even though it seemed harmless, it definitely was not. Other ways we open the door to tormenting spirits are through drug and alcohol abuse; sin; by watching, reading, or listening to evil things; or getting involved with harmful people and events.

My thought as a mother was that if I allowed my children to think that witches, ghosts, and so forth were just fun things, they would be ignorant of how dangerous those things really are. I knew I would not let them experiment with drugs and alcohol, so why would I not protect them from things that could also destroy their spiritual lives, keeping them from God's best and eternal life?

There is another spirit that rips apart believers and churches and harms our witness to the world. It's called a religious spirit. In the book of Acts, chapter 7, verses1–54, Stephen was arrested by the Sanhedrin, and the high priests question him. He gave the historical account of how God worked in the lives of their people, but they were very stubborn and would not listen.

In verse 51, Stephen called them stiff-necked people and told them that they always resist the Holy Spirit. And in verse 52, he recounted how they killed those who predicted the coming of the righteous one. They even killed Him who is Christ the Lord! Verse 54 explains how the religious leaders became very angry at what Stephen said and rushed in to stone him to death. This is clearly a religious spirit. It interferes with the ability of the Holy Spirit to work in people's lives. It is a spirit of laws versus love. It is a prideful, pious spirit. The Pharisees and the Sadducees had this religious spirit. This type of spirit is a hardline legalistic view, and those possessing it believe they are above reproach. They will not embrace the grace Christ offers sinners or the attributes of the Holy Spirit from a loving God. Christ says in Matthew 9:13, "But go and learn what this means: 'I desire mercy, not sacrifice. For I have not come to call the righteous, but sinners.'" For it is by this faith in God through His Son, Jesus Christ, that we believe. It is not a religion of laws but of grace. Laws help us to navigate life in freedom, free from consequence, but by no means save our soul. Only Christ can do that.

We are all sinners; none of us are above reproach. When we begin to think that we are, our pride will open a door for a religious spirit to take hold in our lives. This very thing in those who profess to be Christians has turned off many people from coming to church, reading the Bible, or listening to anything we have to say. Evil comes in many forms. We have to be alert and sober and in a daily relationship with our Lord Jesus to stay clear of it.

My objective is for everyone who reads my work to read the Bible and study it for themselves. Please take whatever you read or hear back to the Word of God in prayer. Ask the Holy Spirit to teach you and help you understand. It is said that knowledge is power. This is absolutely true. What you don't know can hurt you and your family now and for eternity.

My people are destroyed from lack of knowledge. (Hosea 4:6)

It's All about Prayer

Be joyful in hope, patient in affliction, faithful in prayer.
Romans 12:12

I cannot remember a time when I felt totally hopeless. I know that this is because of God, our Creator, in my life and the fact that I was taught to pray. Even before I accepted Jesus Christ into my heart at eight years old, my parents had taught me about the love of God. My mother, especially, talked to me often about prayer. She spoke of how God is always there for us, always listening and wanting to move on our behalf. What a precious gift I received from her.

The one thing I wish my mother would have talked to me about more was how God answered her prayers. She has gone home to be with the Lord, so it's too late for that now. But I often wonder why people don't talk more about their answered prayers. Why are we so afraid to share this precious information? These personal accounts would be very beneficial to others.

Throughout my life, I have prayed and seen God at work. Sometimes He has answered my prayers immediately, like when one of our daughters was in another state and became ill. She was told she must be able to complete the task she was there for or go home. I called on family and friends, and we began praying. Within thirty minutes, her illness went away, and she was able to begin her training. At other times, I feel God is telling me, "Wait. Things have to take place before this prayer can be answered." So weeks and even months may go by until some answer comes. And in response to other prayers, I felt the answer was, "No, that cannot take place as you would desire."

In trying to understand this, I go back to what I know, and that is being a parent. Our children requested things every day, and being twenty-five plus years older and wiser than they, I often answered no. *No* is a really good word in many cases. No kept our children from getting into things they could not handle. It kept them from harm, and it kept them from having it all and becoming full of themselves and prideful. I understand from reading scripture that God, as our parent, works in a similar way.

> Do not be wise in your own eyes; fear the Lord and shun evil. This will bring health to your body and nourishment to your bones. (Proverbs 3:7–8)

I know God knows what is best for me, just like I knew what was best for my children. I have witnessed the powerful presence of God through prayer. I have been totally amazed and in awe of the Lord and what He does when I pray. The wonderful thing about our Father in heaven is that He just doesn't answer our prayers. Very often, He answers them in a way that is above and beyond anything we could imagine.

There was a period in my life when I felt that God did not respond to my constant prayer over a very distressing matter. I must say that those were years of great frustration as I asked Him to move in my situation. I had tried everything I knew to do, and I was left with knowing that only God could change the circumstances. But amid that dark period, there was also inner peace. I was able to go about my life in a joy-in-the-moment kind of day-to-day existence. I can look back and see how God carried me and how He allowed good things and good people to come in and out of my life during that challenging time. He did not allow me to become totally discouraged or feel abandoned.

> Take delight in the Lord, and He will give you the desires of your heart. (Psalm 37:4)

In the end, God did not answer my initial twelve-year prayer, but because I took great joy in His presence, He did give me the desires of my heart. I believe the Lord truly loves to do that for His children. What surprised me was that some of those desires He fulfilled, I had never spoken in prayer or shared with others. They were dreams I'd kept to myself. But my heavenly Father knew what they were.

I must say prayer has been the backbone of my life. It is like eating, drinking water, and sleeping; I need it to survive. Prayer is simply a conversation with God. So when I am communing with God, I feel that He keeps me in an upright position physically, mentally, and spiritually. He is like the chiropractor for my mind, body, and spirit. He keeps me aligned, so I have less pain and consequences. Because of that, I enjoy much happiness. Because I put my trust in Him, He keeps my life in alignment for the very purpose that He put me here.

I also believe God keeps some of our purposes to Himself and reveals them to us a little bit at a time as we mature and are able to handle them. When we begin to evaluate how He answers our prayers and works in our lives—and add that to the wisdom He imparts in us—we can set in motion the very purpose and plan of God. But know this requires us to put those pieces together intentionally, driven by a willing spirit, not just a willing attitude. See the chapter "Effective Bible Study" to understand the difference.

Just like prayer, the best gift we can give ourselves and others is time to be still. Time to think quietly, pray, evaluate, and study the Bible. I know Satan wants to keep us very busy so that we will not have the time to be still and pray. He very much wants to keep us from using the most complex, brilliantly designed receiver-transmitter ever—our brains. The ability to think and connect with God, to pray to the Lord God Almighty, His Son Jesus, and to the Holy Spirit is a danger to the enemy's plan. Simply put, the power of prayer and the power of thought have the power to change the world.

Reasons We Pray

There are many types of prayer for different situations, and you can easily research those. I mainly want to address intercessory prayer. One major reason we pray is to intercede, to bring God into situations in order to break Satan's strongholds and shift the direction things are going. We intercede for people and events in our world, and we ask the Lord to come into our own circumstances to help us.

What we are really doing is going to battle in prayer. The enemy, Satan, would love nothing more than to see us ignore the hurting, accept the things we know are wrong as normal, and walk away from prayer. Satan hopes we will also walk away from our faith in God and reject His Son, Jesus Christ. He wants us to throw up our hands and say, "It's no use!" In the war of the spiritual world, a prayer is a win for God's teams, while a hopeless, defeated attitude is a win for Satan's.

> And pray in the Spirit on all occasions with all kinds of prayers and requests. With this in mind, be alert and always keep on praying for all the Lord's people. (Ephesians 6:18)

Prayer Gives Us Hope

We can live in expectation because we pray. Growing your faith in the Lord through prayer brings a trust and an expectation that fosters hope. Hope that our prayers are taken into consideration and that the Lord will act on our behalf because we pray. Hope is a belief that our situations will someday change for the good.

> Therefore I tell you, whatever you ask for in prayer, believe that you have received it, and it will be yours. (Mark 11:24)

> If you believe, you will receive whatever you ask for in prayer. (Matthew 21:22)

We Glorify God with Our Prayers

God is glorified when we pray with a sincere heart because we are actually acknowledging who He is. We are putting action to our beliefs for we desire to converse with Him. And He so graciously blesses us for it.

Let us acknowledge the Lord; let us press on to acknowledge Him. As surely as the sun rises, He will appear; He will come to us like the winter rains, like the spring rains that water the earth. (Hosea 6:3)

God is glorified when we pray for others. Prayer can be one of the most helpful and life-altering things we can do for another person, and God loves when we care for others.

The king will reply, "Truly I tell you, whatever you did for one of the least of these brothers and sisters of mine, you did for me." (Matthew 25:40)

God is glorified when we pray for our world and all that is happening. I believe when the things that break the Lord's heart begin to break ours, He is glorified because we are becoming more like Him.

He is the Maker of heaven and earth, the sea, and everything in them, He remains faithful forever. He upholds the cause of the oppressed and gives food to the hungry. The Lord sets prisoners free, the Lord gives sight to the blind, the Lord lifts up those who are bowed down, the Lord loves the righteous. The Lord watches over the foreigner and sustains the fatherless and the widow, but He frustrates the ways of the wicked. (Psalm 146:6–9)

God is glorified when He answers our prayers, and with a thankful, sincere heart, we give testimony to those answered prayers. Remember when I asked why people are so afraid to share their answered prayers? I believe Satan hates us giving testimony to answered prayers as much or more than our act of prayer. Why? Because the testimony of what God has done changes lives and dispels Satan's lies. When someone hears a personal testimony, Satan knows there is a very good chance that person may move from his team to God's, therefore glorifying God! I believe life testimonies and those of answered prayers carry a special significance all their own.

Testimonies display God's faithfulness and love in a tangible, Spirit-filled way. Let me explain it in this simple earthly example. When you were a teen, you probably had an actor, singer, or sports figure you would have just about given up all your earthly possessions to meet. Now, say your friend got such an opportunity with this important figure and came to tell you all about the meeting. Would you not hang on every word of his or her experience? Can't you just see how the excitement may have even given you goosebumps and a sense of awe as you listened to your friend's story? It's the same way a testimony of God's great power gets a person's attention! I know that's a silly example, but I hope it gets my point across. A testimony of how God works in us carries a lot more influence than an account of an earthly superstar because God sends His Holy Spirit to be in that testimony and help deliver it. If you are reading this, I encourage you to speak out your prayer victories and your life's testimony. How will anyone ever know or hear it unless you do? How will anyone's life ever be transformed unless you take this simple but powerful step to glorify the Lord God Almighty?

> Therefore, since we are receiving a kingdom that cannot be shaken, let us be thankful, and so worship God acceptably with reverence and awe. (Hebrews 12:28)

> I always thank my God for you because of His grace given you in Christ Jesus. For in Him you have been enriched in every way-with all kinds of speech and with all knowledge-God thus confirming our testimony about Christ among you. (1 Corinthians 1:4–6)

Things to Consider about Prayer

We all have questions about prayer and why some prayers are not answered. All I know is what I have experienced and what I read in the Bible. I am not God, and I will never claim to know all the reasons He answers some prayers and not others. But I believe there are scriptures that may give us clues for some situations. We also must understand that God knows the big picture, the one we cannot see, so His reasons may be unknown to us. We just have to trust that He will work out all things for our good. He sure has in my life. Even in my frustration, I still trust the Lord.

As the heavens are higher than the earth, so are My ways higher than your ways and My thoughts than your thoughts. (Isaiah 55:9)

And we know that in all things God works for the good of those who love Him, who have been called according to His purpose. (Romans 8:28)

The Conditions of Our Souls

If my people, who are called by My name, will humble themselves and pray and seek my face and turn from their wicked ways, then I will hear from heaven, and I will forgive their sin and will heal their land. (2 Chronicles 7:14)

This verse in 2 Chronicles is talking about prayer and a specific group of people, "people who are called by My name." In the Old Testament, it refers to the Jewish people, but it also includes God's people on this side of the cross, who believe and have accepted God's Son, Jesus, into their lives. This verse states that they must humble themselves and to turn from their wicked ways. God cannot abide sin. We, His people, must repent! I believe the need to repent and ask forgiveness is often because we live in a fallen world in which it is impossible to remain sinless.

In the Lord's Prayer, Matthew 6:9 and 12 (NLT) we are instructed to "Pray like this ... and forgive us our sins, as we have forgiven those who sin against us." This means that each time we pray, we are to ask the Lord to forgive our sins. In 2 Chronicles 7:14b, it states, "then I will hear from heaven and I will forgive your sin and heal your land." God promised to answer their prayers after they repented, so this tells us that sin can be a roadblock to answered prayers.

What about the condition of a sinner's soul and God's response to prayer? I firmly believe He hears the prayer of a sinner for we have the simple proof that when a sinner calls on the name of the Lord, asks for forgiveness of his or her sins, and asks to enter His kingdom, God will not turn a deaf ear. He also responds to a believer's prayer interceding on behalf of a sinner because these are prayers coming from a heart of love for another. So be sure to pray for the Holy Spirit to persuade your unsaved family and friends to accept the gift of salvation.

I also want to mention that I don't believe asking for forgiveness when we pray diminishes Christ's sacrifice for our sins on the cross so we can come into His kingdom when we die. I mean that we are simply saying, "I'm sorry, Lord. Cleanse me so I can be in Your presence." You are His child when you accept His Son, Jesus. You are saved by grace, saved from the destruction that comes to some in the afterlife. But just as your child has your DNA that proves you are his or her parent, we know nothing can change the fact that we are God's children, and He is our Father. But we all have times in our relationships that in order to restore that bond and communication, we must say we are sorry and also forgive.

Unforgiveness

Matthew 6:12 and the following verse clearly state that if we want the Lord to forgive us, we must forgive other people. That being said, if the Lord cannot forgive us our sins because of our inability to forgive another, I see that as a roadblock to answered prayer.

> For if you forgive other people when they sin against you,
> your heavenly Father will also forgive you. But if you do
> not forgive others their sins, your Father will not forgive
> your sins. (Matthew 6:14–15)

A Matter of Faith

Are we cemented in our faith, or is it just a once-a-week social assembly that we engage in because it's always been done that way in our families? I just have to say it: Faith is a personal thing. It is between you and God. Nobody keeps you from heaven or sends you to hell but you! So how strong is your faith? What do you actually believe? When we are talking about prayer, it is necessary to have a strong faith that trusts God's ability. This is key.

But when you ask, you must believe and not doubt, because the one who doubts is like a wave of the sea, blown and tossed by the wind. That person should not expect to receive anything from the Lord. Such a person is double-minded and unstable in all they do. (James 1:6–8)

Ouch, harsh words: "Double-minded and unstable in all they do." The question is, are you playing with your faith in God, or have you made a commitment to Him through His Son, Jesus Christ? Are you in or out of what God calls, "His people, called by His name"? One foot in the world and one foot in some form of faith just doesn't cut it. God wants you to be all in for Him!

So because you are lukewarm—neither hot or cold—I am about to spit you out of my mouth. (Revelation 3:16)

Do you pray because you want to commune with the Lord, or do you only pray when you are desperate? The real question is, do you only talk to your Father in heaven when you need something? If you are not in a daily relationship with the Lord, your faith may not be strong enough to trust Him to answer your prayers. You may doubt!

Another way we doubt is by our speech. I have to admit I have been guilty of this, and it's a hard habit to break. It is so very easy to pray for God to heal your headaches, for example, and then later say to someone, "Oh, my head hurts all the time. I just don't know if it will get better or when." I believe we negate our prayers. The head is just one example. We could be praying for world change, salvation for a family member, illness, or whatever, but we cancel our prayers with our mouths. Beware of this stumbling block. So take notice if our doubts are because of lack of faith or we speak it by what we say, we now know that this, too, can become a roadblock to answered prayer.

An Attitude of Gratitude

Sometimes I found myself a little upset when I worked so hard to do good things for someone, and the person was ungrateful. I remember thinking, *Can they not see how hard that was to do and how much it cost me?* I have witnessed that being around a continuously ungrateful person is a little off-putting, to say the least. You cannot do anything to please people like that. They are never thankful for your efforts. Very often they are only pleased with themselves and what they can do. Do you think God may see the human race that way? Do you think when it is one of His own, He is especially grieved? I don't know for sure, of course. I only know what I have felt as a parent.

I know that I was not the least bit encouraged to jump in and do more for my children when I came across an arrogant, ungrateful attitude. I felt like I would only be encouraging bad behavior if I kept giving and doing for them without setting them straight. Setting them straight often led to saying no to some things and withholding others. Sound like unanswered prayer?

The following scriptures make me wonder if God may hold back answering prayers for the same reason. Do you suppose God wonders why people cannot understand how hard it was for Him to give His only Son, Jesus, as a sacrifice for sin? We often need an attitude adjustment, and that is where daily scripture reading and time with His Holy Spirit comes in. The Holy Spirit gently and lovingly realigns our attitudes back to God. So be thankful, humble, loving, and kind. Do not let an ungrateful, prideful spirit be a roadblock to your prayers.

> Do not be anxious about anything, but in every situation,
> by prayer and petition, with thanksgiving, present your
> request to God. (Philippians 4:6)

> When you ask, you do not receive, because you ask with
> wrong motives, that you may spend what you get on your
> own pleasures. (James 4:3)

Pride goes before destruction, a haughty spirit before a fall. (Proverbs 16:18.

> He does not answer when people cry out because of the
> arrogance of the wicked. (Job 35:12)

Powerful Ways to Pray

A prayer can be as simple as praying, "Lord, help!" Or it can be as detailed and involved as binding and loosing, declaring and decreeing. Each part of a prayer life has a particular purpose, and I pray that you, the reader, will begin to use them all. I will hit on the basics from the Bible. I want to give you the quick facts and pray that you will grow to love prayer and study and begin to read more about it. Again, there are many books you can find for in-depth information on prayer. I write about what I know from scripture and experience. I try to make it as simple as possible because I do not believe anything from God has to be too difficult to understand. When in doubt, ask the Holy Spirit to teach you all things and reveal the meaning of them to you.

Let's first talk about some of the things we normally pray about. We often pray for our family, friends, and ourselves. We pray for protection, health, jobs, our nation, our leaders, military, first responders, those struggling, the abused, and so forth. We pray against evil, and we declare life and restoration to people and situations. We often pray for change to occur. In all these ways of prayer, we are basically speaking into situations. Go back to Proverbs 18:21: "The tongue has the power of life and death, and those who love it will eat its fruit." We want to send out good words to make good changes. There is a lot of power in our speech.

> And His incomparably great power for us who believe. That power is the same as the mighty strength He exerted when He raised Christ from the dead and seated Him at His right hand in the heavenly realms. (Ephesians 1:19–20)

> He replied, "Because you have so little faith. Truly I tell you, if you have faith as small as a mustard seed, you can say to this mountain, move from here to there, and it will move. Nothing will be impossible for you." (Matthew 17:20)

In Ephesians we are told we have the same mighty power exerted when He raised Christ from the grave. In Matthew, it talks about speaking to a mountain to move and declaring that nothing is impossible. I believe God has given us the abilities to move mountains in our lives. We are either unaware we can do these things because we do not seek Him and study, or we think it's easier to do nothing and sit back and complain. Hey, I have been there. I know all about it. But now I know scripture and have that close relationship with the Lord. I now know the truth that as a child of God, I have tremendous power through the Holy Spirit to move and change situations by praying and speaking into those situations. So I ask you, "Why not give it a try?"

Speak to disease, and tell it to leave your body now in Jesus's name. Speak to pain or any other impossible situation you may be facing. Tell mountains of things to move, and believe you have the power that the Lord says you do. I know one thing for absolute certainty: If you don't do anything, the changes you desire may never happen. Why not partner with God in prayer and declaration, and watch things change? He is just waiting for you to speak to Him.

> Which of you, if your son asks for bread, will give him a stone? Or if he asks for a fish, will give him a snake? If you then, though you are evil, know how to give good gifts to your children, how much more will your Father in heaven give good gifts to those who ask Him! (Matthew 7:9–11)

Praying Protection and Healing

When we pray for our loved ones, ourselves, and others for protection, we can pray something like this: "I plead the blood of Jesus over my husband and my children for their safety and their health in Jesus's name." I believe the reason we can pray this way is because of Exodus 12:1–13. The blood of the lamb on Passover protected each household that was marked by it.

> The blood will be a sign for you on the houses where you are, and when I see the blood, I will pass over you. (Exodus 12:13a)

When he saw Jesus passing by, he said, "Look, the Lamb
of God!" (John 1:36)

Because of these scriptures, I trust that we have been given the right
as children of God to plead the blood of Jesus over our loved ones, our
homes, and even our businesses. We are symbolically covering them with
the blood of the Lamb that can protect them. When we pray this way, we
are saying, "Lord, I give these people to You. I ask You to cover and protect
them because You are the Lamb of God. Lord, I give You my home and
my business. I put it all in Your hands for they are the means by which I
protect and provide for my family. So I plead the blood of Jesus over them.
In Jesus's name."

Jesus's death and resurrection did not just cleanse us by canceling our
sins. It brought to those who believe healing, protection, and eternal life.
It also broke Satan's hold over us. But Jesus had to spill His blood and be
offered up as the Lamb of God for us to receive these gifts.

> But he was pierced for our transgressions, crushed for our
> iniquities; the punishment that brought us peace was on
> him, and by his wounds we are healed. (Isaiah 53:5)

We can pray, "Lord, Your Word states that by Your stripes we are
healed. I stand on the truth of your Word, and I pray for healing to come
to [name] in Jesus's name."

> We can also pray Psalm 91:1–16 and Isaiah 54:17 over
> them.

Praying Scripture

Just like the example on healing, we can pray scripture over everything in
our lives because God's own words carry great power from above.

> The Spirit gives life; the flesh counts for nothing. The
> words I have spoken to you—they are full of the Spirit
> and life (John 6:63)

93

> These are the words of Him who is holy and true, who
> holds the key of David. What he opens no one can shut,
> and what He shuts no one can open. (Revelation 3:7b)

> For no word from God will ever fail. (Luke 1:37)

When confused about which choice to make, pray something like this: "Lord, Revelation 3:7 states that what door You open, no one can shut, and You shut doors that no one can open. So, Lord, You know what job opportunity I should take, so open the door to the one that is best for me, and close the door on the one that is wrong. In Jesus's name, Amen." You can pray this over many things, even over leaders who need to make important decisions that affect us all. You can also pray for the Lord to open doors for the gospel to reach a nation, state, or city, for revival to come, and to close the doors on any opposition that may come against it.

Pray against evil schemes we see in our world: "He thwarts the plans of the crafty so that their hands achieve no success" (Job 5:12).

You get the idea. Once you start reading the Bible, you will have a wealth of scripture to pray.

Decree or Declare a Thing

> Thou shalt also decree a thing, and it shall be established
> unto thee: and the light shall shine upon thy ways. (Job
> 22:28 KJV)

Speak life into situations: "I decree I will find God's mate for my life." "I decree revival will come to our city." "I decree health and healing will be mine." "I decree a very good solution will present itself for this situation." Whatever the case may be, you are declaring what you want to see happen for the present and the future. Again, life and death are in the power of your tongue.

I want to reiterate the point of Proverbs 18:21. Think of it like this. We are at batting practice, and I am throwing the same ball (Proverbs 18:21, the power of your words) to you over and over again. You miss it the first, second, and even the third time. But when you finally connect with the ball, you achieve your goal of a home run. So here comes another pitch! What we say carries a lot of weight in the spirit world. What you may not realize is that angels and demons also hear those words and follow those commands. So let's keep the angels busy and give the demons the boot. I declare God will win control over my mouth!

Rebuking

> The Lord said to Satan, "The Lord rebuke you, Satan! The Lord, who has chosen Jerusalem, rebuke you! Is not this man a burning stick snatched from the fire?" Zechariah 3:2)

> But even the archangel Michael, when he was disputing with the devil about the body of Moses, did not himself dare to condemn him for slander but said, "the Lord rebuke you!" (Jude 9)

> He said to them, "Go into all the world and preach the gospel to all creation. Whoever believes and is baptized will be saved, but whoever does not believe will be condemned. And these signs will accompany those who believe: In my name they will drive out demons; they will speak in new tongues." (Mark 16:15–17)

> Very truly I tell you whoever believes in me will do the works I have done and they will do even greater things than these, because I am going to the Father. And I will do whatever you ask in my name so that the Father may be glorified in the Son. You may ask anything in my name, and I will do it. (John 14:12–14)

In the verses above, the Lord did the rebuking. But in Mark 16:17 and John 14:12, the Lord gives us authority over the prince of darkness to do what Jesus did and order Satan and his evil spirits to leave.

We are God's people, and we do not have to accept Satan's lies. We do not have to accept a bad report without giving God the opportunity to work through it. We do not have to accept temptation or fear. We simply tell Satan to leave in Jesus's name. We do not have to believe thoughts that we are not good enough, smart enough, or anything along those lines. We believe what God says and declare, "Satan, the Lord rebukes you and your lies. I now tell you to leave in Jesus's name." Let me give you a personal example.

My husband worked third shift. He had left for work and had about a thirty-minute drive. About ten minutes after he left, as I was getting ready for bed, an overwhelming, oppressive fear came over me about his safety. Praise God, it was a one-time thing because it was all-consuming and terrifying. I thought before panicking, *I am not going to accept this!* I did not want anything to happen to him, and I knew enough from studying scripture and spending time with the Lord that I needed to come against this evil spirit of fear. The first thing I did was to reject the thought that something was going to happen to my husband, saying, "I reject this, and the Lord rebukes you, spirit of fear, and I declare that my husband will be safe going to and from work in Jesus's name." Then I began to pray for his protection and continued to declare that he would get to work safely and come home safe. As I was praying, feelings of oppression and fear left. I called him at work, and he was perfectly fine. I simply turned the whole thing over to God and peacefully went to bed. I slept well, and my husband came home without any incidents.

I have often wondered what would have happened had I agreed with that evil spirit of fear. I think I know the answer. I totally believe if we agree with things, we can make them come into being for good or for evil. The truth is, if we allow fear, lies, and temptation to overtake us, it cripples us and can ruin our futures. So don't come into any agreement with negative, harmful thoughts, emotions, or words. Reject them. Rebuke them, and go on about your life in a more positive way.

Binding and Loosing

> Truly I tell you, whatever you bind on earth will be bound
> in heaven, and whatever you loose on earth will be loosed
> in heaven. (Matthew 18:18)

To bind is to restrain. When we bind things in prayer, we are asking the Lord to restrain evil activity, events, and so on. Again, it's all about the power of your words in the heavenly realm. We are simply standing on God's Word. For example: "I bind the plans of the enemy for our nation in Jesus's name." "I bind up the spirit of selfishness over [name] in Jesus's name." "I bind up the spirit of fear that keeps me from traveling, in Jesus's name."

Loosing is about letting something free to shift things. I know we hardly ever use the words *bind* and *loose* in the context of prayer in many churches. But it's in the Bible, and I know that it is important.

I know it is another tool the Lord has given us to use in prayer to change situations. My favorite way to use this is to pray, "I loose love, joy, peace, patience, gentleness, forbearance, self-control and salvation over this nation," or a person. "I loose a good economy." "I loose blessings and favor and protection on my family." I find it fun to pray like this; it feels good to speak these things.

Prayer Language

I would be remiss in writing this prayer chapter if I did not briefly cover the subject of the supernatural prayer language, speaking in tongues. First Corinthians 14:14 tells us, "For if I pray in a tongue, my spirit prays, but my mind is unfruitful." The Holy Spirit speaks through the believer in a language the believer does not know. Some understand that unknown tongues can be used as a prayer language and in an assembly of believers where there are interpreters. Understanding that, the application of tongues can be for two purposes. Whatever the case maybe, it is a manifestation of the Holy Spirit and is one of God's spiritual gifts.

> Now to each one the manifestation of the Spirit is given
> for the common good. To one there is given through

the Spirit a message of wisdom, to another a message of knowledge by means of the same Spirit, to another faith by the same Spirit, to another gifts of healing by that one Spirit, to another miraculous powers, to another prophecy, to another distinguishing between spirits, to another speaking in different kinds of tongues, and to still another the interpretation of tongues. All these are the work of one and the same Spirit, and He distributes them to each one, just as He determines. (1 Corinthians 12:7–11)

For several years, I was confused and not sure what I thought about speaking in tongues. At the time, I was more worldly than spiritual. I was young and caught up in my life and what was fun and good for me. Even though I believed and had accepted Jesus as my Savior, I did not spend time in the scriptures or much time in prayer. Sadly, I regret that I was simply too preoccupied and busy pursuing things other than God.

Some people believe in the gift of tongues; some shut it down altogether, thinking it to be evil. But the Bible talks about it as a natural and beautiful gift that God has given us. He has also given us free will, which I have talked about many times in this book. We are given opportunities and gifts; it is our personal choices as to what we decide to do with them. It is between us and God. We cannot make spiritual choices for anyone other than ourselves. I believe we should not belittle or condemn anyone for using the gifts of the Holy Spirit, or not using them. Because of the following scripture, I suggest we exercise caution and not speak harshly against the gifts of the Spirit either because it is through the Holy Spirit that we operate in them.

And I tell you, every kind of sin and slander can be forgiven, but blasphemy against the Spirit will not be forgiven. Anyone who speaks a word against the Son of Man will be forgiven, but anyone who speaks against the Holy Spirit will not be forgiven, either in this age or in the age to come. (Matthew 12:31–32)

The following scripture points out another reason these gifts may be off-putting to someone. I have to say, I think it is possible for a person to ignore and quiet the Holy Spirit in his or her life and live only in a head-knowledge faith in God versus a heart-driven relationship.

> The person without the Spirit does not accept the things that come from the Spirit of God but considers them foolishness, and cannot understand them because they are discerned only through the Spirit. (1 Corinthians 2:14)

The gift of tongues is often received by those who have a deep desire to be in one accord with God through His Holy Spirit. Sometimes they ask the Holy Spirit for this gift, and other times it is just given to them. This spiritual level of His presence where supernatural gifts are graciously given is called the baptism of the Holy Spirit.

> When you got saved you got the Holy Spirit, the baptism of the Holy Spirit is when He gets you. (Pastor Steve Harman)

Here are just a few of the benefits of praying in tongues:

1. This prayer language connects earth to the heavenly realm.
2. It connects our spirits to God's.
3. It builds up our faith.
4. It helps us pray powerful prayers.
5. It is a language Satan does not understand.

I like Linda Markowitz's, *Fire Up Your Power Tools.* Her book is a wonderful story about how the gift of tongues came to her. She explains this gift in an easy-to-understand but powerful way. It is well worth reading.

This prayer language is nothing to be afraid of; fear does not come from God. It is a wonderful spiritual tool you can use like all the rest I have talked about in this chapter. But it is one to be used only in your private prayer room unless you are at a gathering where someone has the gift of interpretation, and this prayer language is widely embraced.

> If anyone speak in a tongue, two—or at the most three—
> should speak, one at a time, and someone must interpret. If
> there is no interpreter, the speaker should keep quiet in the
> church and speak to himself and to God. (1 Corinthians
> 14:27–28)

This language is life and faith enhancing and powerful in bringing down strongholds. It is a prayer warrior's secret weapon.

> For anyone who speak in a tongue does not speak to
> people but to God. Indeed, no one understands them;
> they utter mysteries by the Spirit. (1 Corinthians 14:2)

> While Peter was speaking these words, the Holy Spirit
> came on all who heard the message. The circumcised
> believers who had come with Peter were astonished that
> the gifts of the Holy Spirit had been poured out even on
> Gentiles. For they heard them speaking in tongues and
> praising God. (Acts 10:44–46)

Do we need these gifts to be able to pray? Absolutely not. The Holy Spirit became a part of you when you became a child of God. But we activate the gifts of the Spirit when we are baptized by the Holy Spirit. In Acts 2:1–4 and in Acts 8:16–17, we see that sometimes God baptizes people with His Holy Spirit immediately. Other times, people lay on hands and pray for each other to receive the baptism of the Holy Spirit: When Paul placed his hands on them, the Holy Spirit came on them, and they spoke in tongues and prophesied (Acts 19:6). If we want this gift or other spiritual gifts, we may ask the Lord to baptize us in His Holy Spirit and grant our request.

Remember, everything we do we are to do in love. So pray out of a heart of love for others and our world in whatever manner the Lord has called you to.

> If I speak in tongues of men or of angels, but do not have
> love, I am only a resounding gong or a clanging cymbal.
> If I have the gift of prophecy and can fathom all mysteries

and all knowledge, and if I have a faith that can move mountains, but do not have love, I am nothing. If I give all I possess to the poor and give over my body to hardship that I may boast, but do not have love, I gain nothing. (1 Corinthians 13:1–3

And now these three remain: faith, hope and love. But the greatest of these is love. (1 Corinthians 13:13)

Eternity without God

Many people have some idea of what will happen when they die. Some believe in heaven and hell, and some do not. One line of thinking is that hell is just life without God. I agree that would be part of it, but I wonder if those people have considered what that scenario might be like.

The Visit

A Fictional Short Story

Helen woke up to the sun shining through her bedroom window and a wonderful summer breeze filling the room. She yawned and said to herself, "What a beautiful summer morning! I had better get up and get going." As she showered and got ready, Helen noticed that her husband had already taken the laundry to the washer. She loved the little things he did for her. He was a very loving man and liked showing her, in so many ways, how much he cared.

Out in the kitchen, her husband and their three children were getting breakfast and talking about their day. "Don't forget to pick me and Tommy up from practice Mom," Timmy said.

"Oh, yeah, Mom or Dad, one of you, I need a ride to play practice tonight," Melanie exclaimed.

"OK you three," Helen said, "we will make sure you all get where you need to go, just like always!" Oh, how Helen loved her family. They were busy, but that was her life. She loved her dog and her flower gardens as well, even though she sometimes found her dog digging in her well-manicured landscape! Life was pretty good, even though she had not embraced the devotion to God that her parents had. Sometimes she felt like maybe she should, "pick up religion," as she called it, but then with their busy schedule and sports on Sunday, she would brush the thought aside and decide to deal with it later, after life had slowed down some.

Out the door they all went, off to school and off to their jobs. Helen worked on the opposite side of town, so her commute was much longer than her husband's. As she was driving along, thinking about the details of her life and the day, a car came speeding out of a side street, striking Helen's car. The impact sent her car spinning out of control. It eventually ran up on the sidewalk, hitting a tree on the other side of the street. The air bag deployed, but Helen was already drifting into unconsciousness from the initial impact on her head and neck.

It all happened so fast, and Helen was only aware of drifting out of her body. She was headed though a black tunnel, void of all things she knew to be normal. All she could think about was that there was nothing pleasant—no laughter, no loved ones, no color or beauty. Just ugliness. *Oh, how I wish I had a cup of coffee and was sitting on my back porch with my family,* she thought. *No, I'm drifting off into a very scary place! What's happening? Where am I going?*

Within seconds, the air around her became hotter than she could ever imagine being able to tolerate. She noticed that the smell was awful; it was burning her lungs. She heard people screaming and crying. There seemed to be no comfort there, no drink or food, no love or beauty. Nothing but fear, panic, and pain. *Why am I here?* she wondered. *This must be hell!* She wondered if God had rejected her or whether she rejected Him? Had she not thought earlier this week about getting around to God someday? Well someday came and claimed her life. *Someday should have been yesterday,* she thought as she cried deeply and painfully, like she never knew was possible. If she had only listened to her parents instead of people who said that God was unimportant, make-believe, and old-fashioned.

Why didn't I trust my parents? They loved me and were only trying to tell me the truth. Why did I believe other people over my own mother and father? Now here I am! Suddenly the things her parents had talked about all those years began to fill her mind as she watched with horror the scene set before her. Without thought, Helen screamed out the name of Jesus. Immediately, she found herself moving backward and away from this horrible place. She was taken to a lush green field with thousands of beautiful wildflowers, where she met an angel. He impressed upon her that her time was not up. She was to return and tell others what she had seen. It was as if time was unavailable; it was here and gone all at the same time. Nothing made earthly sense.

The next thing Helen knew, she was waking up in a hospital room with all her family around. She had been in a coma for several days. The medical staff was not sure she would pull through due to the extent of her injuries and the fact that they had to resuscitate her in the emergency room on arrival.

Groggy and in pain, Helen was acutely aware that she had never prayed with her children. She had never told them about God or what Jesus did on the cross for their sins. What she was once complacent about was now all too real and important. More real than she wanted to admit. She wanted to get up and tell them what she experienced, but she could not. The pain, grogginess, and in ability to speak very well held her back.

But Helen knew she could pray and prepare the way for the discussion that was to come. Then she wondered if her children and husband would think she was being silly and reject her newly found faith. But she knew that she had to try. She had to do her part and let the Lord do his. The angel said to tell, didn't he? That is why she got the second chance, or was it? Maybe it also had something to do with all those prayers her parents had prayed. Maybe God spared her because of them. What it was that brought her back she may never know, but did it matter? At this point, the only thing that mattered was that she gave her life to Christ and told the story of what she experienced.

Even though she needed time to heal and recover, Helen saw her experience as a blessing that brought her time to connect with her Creator; time to reflect and be ever so thankful. For Helen now knew what her mother meant when she talked about hell being absent from the presence of God. In her mind she could see His creation, and they were all the things that she cherished. They were the things that her eyes, ears, nose, and mouth enjoyed on this earth. Now she knew that God made them for our pleasure because He loves us. What she also realized was that even if we don't accept God here on earth, we still get to enjoy His beauty and creation just like all who do believe. It's not God who rejects us; it's us who reject God. Even though the evidence was right before her, Helen had allowed her stubborn spirit to prevail. Even the precious love of her parents did not dissuade her. No, she was the one who did the rejecting, and it almost cost her. She could have been doomed to an unending, horrific future in hell. "No," she said to herself. "God does not send us to hell, We send ourselves!"

> Anyone whose name was not found written in the book of *life was thrown into the* lake of fire. (Revelation 20:15)

> They will throw them into the blazing furnace, where there will be weeping and gnashing of teeth. (Matthew 13:42)

> For since the creation of the world God's invisible qualities—His eternal power and divine nature—have been clearly seen, being understood from what has been made, so that people are without excuse. (Romans 1:20)

A Life-Altering Situation

I thought I was finished with this book when suddenly, my life took a drastic turn. My husband of thirty-four years died of cancer. I have to say this is one of the hardest things I've had to live through. I lost both my parents, in-laws, relatives, and friends, but those deaths were different from losing my soulmate. He may not have been perfect—no one is—but he was perfect for me.

I am writing about this a few months rather than years after his death because I want to write about grief from a fresh perspective. It is not a pleasant situation to be in, but it is one many of us will experience.

How do we prepare for such a life-altering event? We may anticipate how we will handle it and how it will affect us, but in reality, there is nothing that prepares us for how the death of a spouse is going to affect us emotionally, physically, and even spiritually when it actually happens.

My parents were around ninety when they died, and things had not been good for them for a while. I was sad, and I did grieve for a time. I grieved the life I had with them before their minds and bodies failed, when I could still have conversations with them. My parents were very important to me, and I was very grateful for their love, support, and the faith they shared with me. The older I got, the more I treasured them and their wisdom. It was hard to let go of the people they once were but not hard to give them back to God and let go of the suffering, confused people they had become.

I lost a friend to suicide, and that was hard in a different way. It was a sudden, unanticipated death, and one that was hard to comprehend. The pain and grief from that death took a long time to work through. I had texted my friend that week, and she did not respond. I brushed it aside, thinking she was just busy. Afterward, I was left with some regret about things I didn't do or say. Those thoughts began to eat away at me, and I had to give it all to God. Otherwise, I knew it would tarnish the wonderful memories I had of my friend. Such negative feelings left unchecked begin to negate the blessings God gives us. The people in our life are truly blessings. This I know in my heart. I was definitely blessed with many years of her friendship, laughter, and generosity. And for that, I will forever be grateful.

The death of a child and the seemingly unbearable grief it must bring, is not something I can write about. I have not lost one of my children, and I pray I never do. I pray I exit this world before they do. I know it must be unimaginably hard on parents and family members who lose a child. My heart goes out to them.

I now know what it's like to lose a spouse. As I write this, I wish with everything in me that I did not know this grief. It is so different from any other grief I've experienced because of the closeness of our relationship. My husband, Mark, was my everyday person. He was the love of my life. We walked in sync with each other everyday for thirty-four years. A year ago, on Valentine's Day, Mark found a poster online and framed it as a gift for me. It reads, "When I tell you I love you I don't say it out of habit or to make conversation. I say it to remind you that you are the best thing that ever happened to me."

I often said Mark and I had a marriage that many people only wished for. We were committed to our relationship and enjoyed making life as good as it could be for each other. We also embraced our individualities and time spent on our own each day doing the things we enjoyed. But then we would spend quite a bit of time together, doing things as a couple. We sincerely enjoyed each other's company. There would be times we talked for hours and then times we never said a word. It was comfortable and casual.

It is so hard to accept that all that is gone. Knowing I will not hear his voice or feel his hand on mine anymore. We will never again enjoy vacations, holidays, or birthdays with our family or do any of the things we loved to do together. All the plans and dreams we had ended abruptly. It's as if a surgeon cut away a vital part of me, and now I am forced to learn to limp along without it.

I'm amazed by how the grief has overtaken me. I have never felt so out of control in all my life. Not only by the grief, but also by all I have to do in response. I feel like I have been in a fog since it happened. Many people who have lost a spouse tell me it just takes time, and everyone's grieving period is different. Some say after about a year they realized that the grief fog had lifted, and they felt better.

> Be merciful to me, Lord, for I am in distress; my eyes
> grow weak with sorrow, my soul and body with grief.
> (Psalm 31:9)

Perhaps if we didn't have the ability to grieve, we wouldn't have a heart of compassion. Grieving is one of our final expressions of love. Sadly, people sometimes don't realize how much they love someone until they are gone. I think God gave people the ability to grieve as a way of releasing the pain. For me, I often release the pain with my tears, but it seems to happen a little less with each month that goes by. I think it's because I'm getting a little more accustomed to this permanent change in my life. But it's not that I miss Mark any less. I am choosing to switch my mind from my loss to joy knowing he is free from the pain and suffering he was going through. I choose to see a vision of him being held in the arms of Jesus, happy in the company of so many people who have gone before us.

When I decided to write about my experience, I asked myself, "Can grief be good?" My initial thought was no. Then I began to look at it from all angles. Grief doesn't feel good; it's painful. What is it they say about exercise? "No pain, no gain!" Can that be also be true about grief? I came to the conclusion that it is a good and necessary part of life. Working through hard things helps us grow as human beings. We become more sympathetic to human struggle and tragedy. We become more like the people God intends for us to be, people who can offer comfort and care to others because we have walked the same path. Without pain, we don't grow. Without growth, we tend to stay in ourselves, concerned only with our own lives.

> Praise be to the God and Father of our Lord Jesus Christ, the Father of compassion and the God of all comfort, who comforts us in all our troubles, so that we can comfort those in any trouble with the comfort we ourselves receive from God. For just as we share abundantly in the sufferings of Christ, so also our comfort abounds through Christ. (2 Corinthians 1:3–5)

Grief makes us cry out to God. I feel at times as if I am in over my head. I am in pain and confused about how to move forward. I need God's help to get me through this. Psalm 23:4 (NKJV) reads, "Yea, though I walk through the valley of the shadow of death, I will fear no evil for you are with me; your rod and your staff, they comfort me." That shadow of death, that darkest valley (as referred to in the NIV version), is not just for the person passing into the next life. That same shadow and valley are what we who are left behind must walk through as well.

I believe the rod/staff in this verse represents God's Word. The shepherd used his rod/staff to guide the sheep, move them away from danger, and keep them comfortable and safe. So does the Bible guide and comfort us in our times of pain and sorrow. I found it easier to listen to the Bible being read than to read it in my early grieving period. I felt so bad, but the comfort was there. Spiritual music was wonderfully comforting to me as well.

I'm going to be totally real here. Out of my grief, I have had to release my disappointment to God and ask for His forgiveness. I cannot say I have been mad at God for not healing my husband, but I have had moments of disappointment. Note this important fact: Allowing disappointment to take root leads to disbelief, and that's a dangerous path to go down. Satan is only too happy to walk us there and gain strongholds in our lives. I knew I had to repent and return to prayer and scripture, which I found uncharacteristically difficult to do early in.

What seems to be happening is that I feel my human side breaking apart. But my spiritual side, that trust, is holding me steadfast in this storm. My relationship with God is very strong, and I know He understands and can handle extreme emotions. The rope to my anchor is trust, a trust I established long ago and have built my life around. I trust my family and my future to the Lord, who is my anchor. Even though my husband was not healed here on earth, he is healed in heaven. For that I am grateful and find much peace.

Out of this tragedy, I noticed that many people were touched by my husband's life and faith. There was a testimony there that was more powerful than life. There was also a reminder that it can all be taken away quickly and to cherish every moment we have with the ones we love. His death also spoke to some of an urgent need to establish a relationship with the Lord before it's too late.

To me, it was a stark reminder that all the material things we humans think we need are just cold, hard objects. I thought I would find comfort in my husband's things. I did not. I would drive his truck or hold his clothes, but I found no comfort there. The person who made them important was not in them or using them anymore, so I found them meaningless to me. This, too, surprised me.

I feel my husband and I went through an ugly cancer battle, and my husband died on the battlefield. I did not get to bring him home. It will take some time to recover, but while I am healing, I can see how God is working things out for me. I felt His love and presence even in the beginning, when I did not feel like reading scripture or praying more than a few words.

He says to me to rest, heal, and He will help me recover. "He restores my soul" (Psalm 23:3 NKJV). He has sent wonderful people to help me in many tangible ways. Their acts of kindness and compassion renew my faith in the human race. It brings a little joy amid great sadness. All these people are being the hands and feet of God, whether they know it or not.

I am living through a storm. This storm will last as long as it lasts. I have to hunker down and hold onto the rope to my anchor until it passes. I look forward to the future, when the sunshine reappears, and my life feels less cloudy. It will happen. God promises to never leave me or forsake me as in Hebrews 13:5.

The Lord is a refuge for the oppressed, a stronghold in times of trouble. Those who know your name trust in you, for you, Lord, have never forsaken those who seek you. (Psalm 9:9–10)

As I have been writing about being in a storm, the Lord reminded me of this song I loved from 1994. It says it all. I'm so thankful God brought it to mind. I am comforted by it once again.

I have journeyed through the long, dark night out on the open sea. By faith alone, sight unknown and yet His eyes were watching me.

Chorus:

The anchor holds, though the ship is battered, the anchor holds though the sails are torn. I have fallen on my knees as I faced the raging seas, the anchor holds, in spite of the storm.

I've had visions, I've had dreams, I've even held them in my hand. But I never knew they would slip right through like they were only grains of sand.

Chorus:

I have been young, but I am older now and there has been beauty that these eyes have seen. But it was in the night through the storms of my life Oh, that's where God proved His love to me.

Chorus

("The Anchor Holds," by Ray Boltz, used by permission Ray Boltz Music/Shepherd Boy Music 2021.)

If you love people, you will have grief and heartache. I would rather love one thousand people and lose them all than to never love people and have them love me. I have so many wonderful memories made with the people I have loved. These memories bring me great joy. If I had never put myself out there, loved, and followed God's path to people, my heart and my memory book would be empty. That would be more sorrowful than the loss of a loved one.

The wonderful news is, if we are all in the family of God, believing in His Son, Jesus, we will see each other again, and we can have the assurance that our loved ones are in a wonderful place! You'll see when you get to heaven yourself.

An Invitation

If you have read my book and have not accepted Jesus into your heart, I pray you choose to make this very important decision.

Steps to Salvation

- Repent: Ask God to forgive your sins.

Repent means to feel or express your sincere regret about your wrongdoing or sin. When you truly repent, you change your mind, which leads to a change of heart and behavior.

> I tell you no! But unless you too repent, you too will all perish. (Luke 13:5)

- Believe and voice your desire to come to Christ and receive the gift of salvation.

> If you declare with your mouth, "Jesus is Lord," and believe in your heart that God has raised Him from the dead, you will be saved. (Romans 10:9)

- Pray a prayer of salvation similar to this:

    Jesus, I believe You are the Son of God, who died for my sins and rose from the grave so that I might have eternal life. I ask You to come into my life and forgive my sins and accept me into Your kingdom as Your son [daughter]. I want to make You Lord of my life. In Jesus's name I pray. Amen.

If you prayed that prayer and meant it, you are now a child of God. Welcome to the family of believers! Now begin by asking the Lord to help you forgive others in order to rid yourself of any anger or bitterness you may have. This is very difficult, if not impossible to do without God's help as stated, "apart from me, you can do nothing" (John 15:5b). This is a very important first step because of Matthew 6:14–15.

Thank you for reading my book. I leave you with this beautiful blessing over your life:

    The Lord bless you and keep you; the Lord make His face shine on you and be gracious to you; the Lord turn His face toward you and give you peace. (Numbers 6:24–26)

Notes

Chapter: "A Solid Foundation for Life"

"My Hope Is Built on Nothing Less," written in 1834 by Edward Mote (1797–1874), music composed for the text in 1863 by William Bradbury (1816–1863).

Artwork created for this book by artist Shelly Stout:

Poem: "Reflections of Myself," Sally's favorite scripture, Philippians 4:13, and poem: "Once Again."

Chapter: "Effective Bible Study"

The Divine Mentor, by Wayne Cordeiro, author and pastor of New Hope Church and College, Eugene, Oregon. Published by Bethany House Publishing, October 1, 2008. All quotes and endorsements by Wayne Cordeiro are used with written permission.

Chapter: "Fear Lies and Jail Cells"

"Fear Is a Liar," by Zach Williams, written by Jason Ingram, Jonathan Smith, and Zach Williams. Provident Label Group, 2017.

Chapter: "Walking in the Truth, Led by the Spirit of God"

"God Only Knows," by For King & Country, written by Josh Kerr, Jordan Reynolds. Word Entertainment, 2019.

Chapters: "Where Is True Happiness," "The Secrets to Enduring Love," and "It's All about Prayer."

Quotes used with written permission by Pastor Steven S. Harman, ThD, retired church plant pastor, current volunteer missionary with A Time to Revive and Revive Ohio Ministries.

Chapter: "It's All about Prayer."

Fire Up Your Power Tools: A Practical Handbook for Using the Gift of Tongues. by Linda Markowitz. Published by Linda Markowitz Ministries, 2018.

Chapter: "A Life-Altering Situation."

Lyrics to the song "The Anchor Holds," used by permission, Ray Boltz Music/Shepherd Boy Music, 2021. Song released in 1994, performed by Ray Boltz.

Printed in the United States
by Baker & Taylor Publisher Services